SLOWCOOKER
EASY

SLOWCOOKER EASY

OVER 70 DELICIOUSLY SIMPLE RECIPES

hamlyn

SARA LEWIS

First published in Great Britain in 2006 by Hamlyn, a division of
Octopus Publishing Group Ltd,
2–4 Heron Quays, London E14 4JP

Copyright © 2006 Octopus Publishing Limited

ISBN-13: 978-0-600-61512-5
ISBN-10: 0-600-61512-X

A CIP catalogue record for this book is available
from the British Library

Printed in China

10 9 8 7 6 5 4 3 2 1

Notes

Standard level spoon measures are used in all the recipes
1 tablespoon = one 15 ml spoon
1 teaspoon = one 5 ml spoon

Both metric and imperial measurements are given for the recipes. Use one set
of measures only, not a mixture of both.

A few recipes include nuts and nut derivatives. Anyone with a known nut allergy
must avoid these. It is advisable for people with known allergic reactions to
nuts and nut derivatives and those who may be particularly vulnerable to avoid
dishes made with nuts and nut oils. It is also prudent to check the labels of
pre-prepared ingredients for the possible inclusion of nut derivatives.

Read your slow cooker manual before you begin and preheat the slow cooker
if required according to the manufacturer's instructions. Because slow cookers
vary slightly from manufacturer to manufacturer, check recipe timings with the
manufacturer's directions for a recipe using the same main ingredient.

All the recipes for this book were tested in slow cookers with a working
capacity of 2.5 litres (4 pints), total capacity of 3.5 litres (6 pints).

Contents

Introduction

We all want to eat healthily, but at times this can seem impossible. The pressures of running a home and, probably, holding down a job, can make spending time in the kitchen the last thing we want to do when we get home. A call to return to home cooking and leave the nutritionally low, chilled ready meals on the supermarket shelves may seem to be flying in the face of experience. But home cooking needn't mean spending hours slaving away in the kitchen. Just 15–20 minutes are all that are needed to prepare a tasty meal that can be left to simmer for 8–10 hours while you get on with your life.

A slow cooker is ideal for families because the supper can be put on in the morning, after the children have gone to school, so that a warm, tasty meal is ready in the late afternoon or early evening, when you and the children are most tired. If you work unsocial hours or on shifts you can put on a

meal before you go to work, so that a meal is waiting when the rest of the family get home. Retired people can leave their supper to cook while they spend the day engaged in more rewarding activities.

Why slow cook?

Food that has been slowly cooked is packed with flavour. When microwave ovens first became widely available they captured everyone's imagination as the answer to our busy lives. But the reality is that food cooked in a microwave is often tasteless and lacking in colour, and most of us now use our microwave ovens for little more than defrosting and reheating foods.

Once a slow cooker is turned on, the food can be left to bubble gently, completely unattended. Because it cooks so slowly, there is no danger that the food will boil dry, spill over or burn on the bottom.

Foods from around the world

The recipes in this book have been inspired by foods from around the world, and they contain mellow spice blends from the Far East, India, Morocco and the Mediterranean and ingredients ranging from pesto, tamarind paste and harissa to aromatics, such as star anise, fennel, cumin and coriander, along with favourite flavourings, such as garlic, wine and fresh herbs.

There is something for everyone, from steaming bowls of soup to new family favourites such as Moroccan Seven Vegetable Stew (see page 73), Turkey Carbonnade with Polenta Squares (see page 92) and Summer Garden Pie (see page 93). For easy entertaining, why not try Peppered Venison

Fry foods first for added flavour when making a casserole or hotpot and always add boiling hot stock.

with Gorgonzola Scones (see page 98), Pot-roast Guinea Fowl with Salsa Verde (see page 90) or Feta Tiganito (see page 102)? As a finale, it would be hard to beat Sticky Toffee Apple Pudding (see page 108) or Mini Coffee Sponge Puddings with Coffee Liqueur (see page 133), with a soft, just melting chocolate centre. In summer you could offer Nectarine Compote with Orange Mascarpone (see page 119).

Not just for stews
A slow cooker is, of course, perfect for making slow-cooked meaty or vegetable casseroles, but it can also be used to steam puddings. The basin can be put directly on to the base of the slow cooker pot – there is no need for a trivet – and boiling water added to the pot until it comes halfway up the basin. Because there is no evaporation you will not need to remember to top up the water or return to find that the pot has boiled dry.

When water is added to the pot, a slow cooker can also be used as a bain marie or water bath to cook baked custards, pâtés or terrines. You can also pour alcoholic or fruit juice mixtures into the pot and heat them to make warming hot party punches or hot toddies, which can be ladled out of the slow cooker pot as required.

The slow cooker pot can also be used to make chocolate or cheese fondues, preserves, such as lemon curd or simple chutneys, and even to boil up bones or a chicken carcass to make into stock.

Money saving
Slow cookers use about the same amount of electricity as an electric light bulb, so they are cheap to run. Moreover, the long, slow cooking transforms even the toughest cheapest cuts of meat into dishes

You can make much more than just a casserole in a slow cooker. Use it as a steamer or water bath too.

that melt in the mouth, and the meat quite literally falls off the bone. Inexpensive dried beans, lentils and split peas also cook beautifully in tasty spiced or tomato sauces. Just remember to soak the beans and peas and boil them first.

Students in shared accommodation or young couples struggling with high mortgages will find slow cookers invaluable when trying to keep to a strict food budget. In addition, they are environmentally friendly: Why turn on the oven for just one dish when you can save on fuel by using the slow cooker?

Getting started

Choose a medium-sized oval or round slow cooker if you are preparing meals for a family of four.

Nothing could be easier than using a slow cooker, but if you are thinking of buying one for the first time, there are a few guidelines to bear in mind.

What size of slow cooker is best?

Slow cookers are measured by their total capacity, and there are three sizes. The size is usually printed on the packaging, together with the working capacity or the maximum space for food:

• For two people: a mini oval cooker with a maximum capacity of 1.5 litres (2½ pints) and a working capacity of 1 litre (1¾ pints).

• For four people: *either* a round *or* the more versatile oval cooker with a total capacity of 3.5 litres (6 pints) and a working capacity of 2.5 litres (4 pints).

• For six people: *either* a large oval cooker with a total capacity of 5 litres (8¾ pints) and a working capacity of 4 litres (7 pints) *or* the extra large round cooker with a total capacity of 6.5 litres (11½ pints) with a working capacity of 4.5 litres (8 pints).

Surprisingly, the very large slow cookers cost only a little more than the middle-sized models, and it is easy to be swept along, thinking that the larger cookers offer better value for money. Unless you have a big family or like to cook large quantities so that you have enough supper for one meal with extra portions to freeze, you will probably find that they are too big for your everyday needs.

The best and most versatile slow cooker is an oval one, which is ideal for cooking a whole chicken, has ample room for a pudding basin or four individual pudding moulds and is capacious enough to make soup for six portions.

Preheating your slow cooker

It is important to read the handbook that comes with your slow cooker before you begin cooking. Some manufacturer's recommend preheating the cooker on the high setting for a minimum of 20 minutes before food is added. Others, however, recommend that the slow cooker is heated only when it is filled with food.

How full should the pot be?

A slow cooker pot must be used only when it contains liquid, and ideally it should be no less than half full. Aim for the three-quarter full mark, or, if you are making soups, make sure that the liquid is no higher than 2.5 cm (1 inch) from the top.

You need to half-fill a slow cooker when you are cooking meat, fish or vegetable dishes, but joints of meat should take up no more than two-thirds of the space. If you are using a pudding basin you must make sure that there is a 2 cm (¾ inch) space all the way round or, if you are using an oval slow cooker, 1 cm (½ inch) at the narrowest point.

Heat settings

All slow cookers will have 'high', 'low' and 'off' settings, and some models may also have 'medium', 'warm' or 'auto' setting. The high setting will generally take only half the time of the low setting when a diced meat or vegetable casserole is cooking. This can be useful if you plan to eat at lunchtime or get delayed in starting the casserole. Both settings will reach just below 100°C (212°F), or boiling point, during cooking, but this temperature is reached more quickly on the high setting.

Using a combination of settings can be useful, and it is recommended by some manufacturers at the beginning of cooking. If your slow cooker is very full, cook on high for 30 minutes at the beginning of cooking to raise the temperature of the casserole quickly and then turn it to low for the remaining time. This can be done automatically if your model has an auto setting, when the cooker reduces the temperature automatically by means of a thermostat. This is ideal if you are rushing out to work.

Alternatively, increasing the temperature from low to high at the end of cooking can be useful if you want to thicken a casserole at the end of cooking with cornflour, add extra green vegetables or reheat soups that you have puréed and returned to the pot.

The warm setting is suitable once the maximum cooking time has been reached, and it will keep the food 'on hold', which is useful if guests are late. The warm setting is not essential, however, because the low setting will not cause foods to spoil unless they are rice based.

What is best at what setting?

Low
- Diced meat or vegetable casseroles
- Chops or chicken joints
- Soups
- Egg custard desserts
- Rice dishes
- Fish dishes

High
- Sweet or savoury steamed puddings or sweet dishes that include a raising agent (self-raising flour or baking powder)
- Pâtés or terrines
- Whole chickens, guinea fowls or pheasants, gammon joints or half a shoulder of lamb

Timings

All the recipes in the book include a span of cooking times, which means that the dish will be tender and ready to eat at the lower time but can be left without spoiling for an extra hour or two, so there is no need to worry if you get delayed at work, stuck in traffic or bogged down in a do-it-yourself project.

If you want to speed up or slow down cooking times for diced meat or vegetable casseroles so that they fit around your plans better, adjust the heat settings and timings as suggested below:

Cook on Low	Cook on Medium	Cook on High
6–8 hours	4–6 hours	3–4 hours
8–10 hours	6–8 hours	5–6 hours
10–12 hours	8–10 hours	7–8 hours

Note: These timings were taken from the Morphy Richards slow cooker instruction handbook. Do not change timings or settings for fish, whole joints or dairy dishes.

Using your slow cooker for the first time

Before you start to use the slow cooker, put it on the work surface, somewhere out of the way, and make sure that the flex is tucked around the back of the machine and does not trail over the front of the work surface or near the hob.

The outside of the slow cooker does get hot, so warn all members of your family, and don't forget to use oven gloves when you are lifting the pot out of the housing. Carefully lift the slow cooker pot out of the housing and put it on to a heatproof mat on the table or work surface.

If your slow cooker lid has a vent in the top, make sure that the slow cooker is not put under an eye-level cupboard, or the steam may catch someone's arm as they reach into the cupboard.

Preparing food for the slow cooker

Meat

Slow-cooked meaty casseroles or stews are obvious choices for a slow cooker. There is no danger that the food will boil dry, and the lengthy cooking time means that the meat will be beautifully tender. For even cooking, make sure that all the pieces of meat are cut to the same size and press them below the surface of the liquid before cooking begins.

You can cook a whole chicken, guinea fowl or pheasant, even a small gammon joint or half a shoulder of lamb, in an oval slow cooker pot, but these should only be cooked on high, unlike diced meat or smaller chicken thigh or drumstick joints, which may be cooked on high, medium or low.

Fish

Fish can also be cooked in the slow cooker. Either cut it into pieces and bake in a rich tomato or vegetable sauce or poach a larger piece, such as a 500 g (1 lb) salmon fillet, in a wine and stock mixture. The slow, gentle cooking means that the fish will not break up or overcook. Make sure that the fish is covered by the liquid so that it cooks evenly.

Do not add shellfish until the last 15 minutes of cooking and make sure that the cooker is set to high. If you use frozen fish, make sure it has completely thawed before use.

Brown diced meat in a little oil or oil and butter to seal in the flavour before slow cooking.

Lower larger pieces of fish or pudding basins into the slow cooker using a long folded strip of foil.

Vegetables

Surprisingly, root vegetables can take longer to cook than meat. If you are adding them to a meaty casserole, make sure that you cut the vegetables into pieces that are a little smaller than the meat. Again, try to keep all the vegetable chunks the same size so that they cook evenly. Press the vegetables and the meat below the surface of the liquid before cooking commences.

Pasta and rice

Pasta tends to go soggy if it's added at the beginning of a recipe. For best results, cook the pasta separately in a saucepan of boiling water and mix it into the casserole just before serving. Small pasta shapes, such as macaroni or shells, can be added to soups 30–45 minutes before the end of cooking.

Basmati and ordinary white long-grain rice can be used in slow cookers, but you will get better results with easy-cook rice, which has been partially cooked during manufacture. Some of the starch has been

washed off, making it less sticky when cooked. Allow a minimum of 250 ml (8 fl oz) water for each 100 g (3½ oz) of easy-cook rice or up to 500 ml (17 fl oz) for risotto rice.

Pulses and lentils

Dried pulses must be soaked overnight in plenty of cold water before use. Drain them, then put them in a saucepan with fresh water and bring to the boil. Boil rapidly for 10 minutes, then drain or add with the cooking liquid to the slow cooker (see the individual recipes for details). Pearl barley and red, Puy or green lentils do not need soaking overnight, but if you are unsure, always check the instructions on the packet.

Cream and milk

Cream and milk can be added but generally only at the beginning of cooking in rice pudding or baked egg custard dishes. Use full-fat milk or double cream because they are less likely to separate.

If you are making soup add the milk at the very end, after the soup has been puréed. Stir cream into soups just 15 minutes before the end of cooking or swirl it over the soup before serving.

Thickening stews and casseroles

Casseroles can be thickened in the same ways as if you were cooking conventionally. Add the flour after searing meat or frying onions, then gradually mix in the stock. Alternatively, add cornflour mixed with a little water 30–60 minutes before the end of cooking or pour off the liquid from the cooked dish into a pan and boil it on the hob until reduced.

Because the liquid does not evaporate during cooking, as it would on the hob, there is no need to lift the lid and check on a stew's progress or top up with stock during cooking. You may find that you can use slightly less stock than you would normally do, but remember that it is important that the meat or vegetables are covered with stock so that they cook evenly.

Getting organized

If you plan to switch on the slow cooker before you go out to work in the morning, you may find it helpful to semi-prepare the dish to be cooked the night before. Chop the onion and seal it in a small plastic bag. Put diced vegetables in an airtight plastic container with a little water, then use this water to add to the slow cooker pot. Dice or slice meat and wrap it in clingfilm or kitchen foil.

Keep all the foods in the refrigerator, then brown them in the morning, while the slow cooker heats up, if your model requires this. Add boiling water to a low-salt stock cube with any vegetable soaking liquid or heat up the stock in the frying pan, after sealing the meat. Transfer the ingredients to the slow cooker pot, add the lid to cover and leave to cook while you are out.

In most of the savoury recipes in this book the ingredients are browned first in a frying pan to improve both their appearance and taste, then thickened, either with flour before they are added to the slow cooker pot or with a little cornflour at the end of cooking.

If you prefer to skip the browning stage, simply add the diced, sliced or minced meat or chicken pieces straight from the refrigerator to the slow cooker pot and cover with boiling stock. You will need to increase the minimum cooking time, adding an extra 2–3 hours if cooking the food on low. Do not be tempted to lift the lid during the first half of cooking or you will need to add an extra 20 minutes to the cooking time. Thicken the casserole at the end with a little cornflour mixed to a paste with water, then cook on high for 30 minutes.

Whether or not you brown the ingredients first, make sure you always add **hot** liquid to the pot.

Do I need any special equipment?

You will probably already have all the equipment you need, although if you are buying a new slow cooker why not treat yourself to a new nonstick frying pan for preparing foods before slow cooking?

It's likely that you will already have a 1.25 litre (2¼ pint) basin for steamed puddings, such as the

You may find that you use slightly less stock as there is no risk of evaporation or the stew boiling dry.

Rosemary Pudding with Mushrooms and Chestnuts (see page 105) or Rum and Raisin Spotted Dick (see page 110). If you have one that is slightly larger, use this, but check that it will fit in your slow cooker before you begin. For recipes such as Bobotie (see page 46), Sticky Toffee Apple Pudding (see page 108), Sticky Glazed Banana Gingerbread (see page 126) or Marbled Chocolate and Vanilla Cheesecake (see page 123) you will need either a soufflé-style dish that is 14 cm (5½ inches) across and 9 cm (3½ inches) high or a straight-sided round dish with a capacity of 1.25 litres (2¼ pints).

The individual puddings, such as the Black Cherry and Chocolate Puddings (see page 112) or the Mini Coffee Sponge Puddings with Coffee Liqueur (see page 133), will require four individual metal moulds, each with a capacity of 200 ml (7 fl oz). Small coffee cups also make good moulds for the Lemon Custard Creams (see page 124), and six cups will fit snugly side by side in an oval slow cooker pot. Again, check that your chosen containers will fit inside your slow cooker before you begin.

Adapting your own recipes

If you want to try some of your own favourite recipes in your slow cooker, you should first look at a similar recipe in this book to give you an idea of the quantity that will fit in the slow cooker pot and the appropriate timing for the main ingredient. Because a slow cooker cooks food gently and evenly you will almost certainly need to reduce the amount of liquid. Begin by using just half the amount of hot liquid specified in the original recipe and then increase it as needed, pressing foods beneath the surface of the liquid and upping the amount as required until they are just covered. Recipes that contain fresh tomatoes will turn to pulp during cooking, so you will not need quite so much liquid.

The steam condenses on the lid of the slow cooker and returns to the pot so there is no danger that food will boil dry. If you find you have reduced the amount of liquid too much, add a little more boiling stock or water at the end of cooking to compensate.

Tip

- **To lift a hot basin easily out of the slow cooker you can buy macramé string pudding basin bags, but do make sure that they will fit a 1.25 litre (2¼ pint) basin before you buy. Alternatively, tear off two long pieces of foil. Fold each into thirds to make a long, narrow strap. Lay one on top of the other to make a cross, then sit the pudding basin in the centre. Lift up the straps and carefully lower the basin into the slow cooker pot.**

It is usually best to add milk or cream at the end of the recipe unless the recipe uses the slow cooker pot as a bain marie or water bath with hot water poured around a cooking dish. Rice pudding is the exception to this rule, and you should use full-fat milk and not semi-skimmed or skimmed milk. Refer to individual recipes in the book for guidance.

Changing the recipes to suit a smaller or larger slow cooker

All the recipes in this book have been tested in a standard slow cooker with a total capacity of 3.5 litres (6 pints). Larger 5 litre (8¾ pint), six-portion sized cookers or tiny 1.5 litre (2½ pint), two-person cookers are also available. To adapt the recipes in this book simply halve for two portions or add half as much again to the recipe, keeping the timings the same. All the recipes made in pudding basins, soufflé dishes or individual moulds may also be cooked in a larger slow cooker for the same amount of time.

Using the slow cooker in conjunction with a freezer

Most of the soups and stews in this book may be frozen, and if you live on your own, freezing individual portions can be a great time saver. After all, it takes little extra effort to make a casserole for four than for two. Defrost portions in the refrigerator overnight or at room temperature for 4 hours, then reheat thoroughly in a saucepan on the hob or in the microwave on full power.

Quick tips

• You can make so much more than casseroles in the slow cooker. Try steamed puddings, baked custards, hot toddies, even cakes, chutneys and preserves.

• Always check that the joint, pudding basin, soufflé dish or individual moulds will fit into your slow

cooker pot before you begin to prepare the ingredients to avoid later frustration.

• Foods cooked in a slow cooker must contain some liquid.

• If you have an electric hand blender, you can purée soups while they are still in the slow cooker pot but take care that you do not knock the edges of the pot.

• Foods will not brown during cooking, so lift the slow cooker pot out of the housing and transfer it to a preheated grill or oven with a grill element. Alternatively, use a cook's blowtorch if you have one.

• Don't be tempted to keep lifting the lid and stirring the food while it is cooking in the slow cooker. Because the food only bubbles gently, even on the highest setting, there is no need to make sure it is not sticking, burning or boiling over. **Every time you lift the lid you add 20 minutes to the cooking time.**

Caring for your slow cooker

If you treat it with care you might find that your machine will last twenty years or more, seeing you through your college days right up until you have a family or through retirement.

Although it is tempting to pop the slow cooker pot and lid into the dishwasher, they do take up a lot of space. Also, you should check with your manual first, because not all slow cookers are dishwasher proof. The slow cooker's heat is so controllable that it is not like a saucepan with burnt-on grime to contend with. Simply lift the slow cooker pot out of its housing, fill it with hot soapy water and leave to soak for a while. Turn off the controls, pull out the plug and allow the machine itself to cool down before cleaning the housing. Wipe the inside with a damp cloth, removing any stubborn marks with a little cream cleaner. Wipe the outside of the machine and the controls with a dishcloth, then buff them up with a duster. Chrome fittings can be sprayed with a little multi-surface cleaner and buffed up with a duster. **Never immerse the machine in water to clean it.**

If you are storing the slow cooker in a cupboard, make sure it is completely cold before you put it away.

Keep safe

• If you are using dried beans, always soak them overnight in cold water and boil them rapidly in a saucepan of fresh water for 10 minutes before you add them to the slow cooker pot. Lentils do not need pre-soaking or boiling.

• Always make sure that frozen food is thawed thoroughly before you add it to the slow cooker, although some frozen vegetables, such as peas and broad beans, can be added without thawing.

• Raw foods that have been taken out of the freezer, thawed and cooked in the slow cooker pot can be returned to the freezer once cooled.

• Add well-rinsed shellfish at the end of cooking in the slow cooker and cook the mixture on high for 15 minutes to make sure that it is piping hot.

• If you are cooking a joint of meat, make sure that it does not fill more than the lower two-thirds of the slow cooker pot. Completely cover the meat with hot liquid. Always check that the joint of meat is fully cooked before serving, either by using a meat thermometer or by inserting a skewer through the thickest part of the joint or through the thickest part of the leg into the breast if you are cooking a whole chicken, guinea fowl or pheasant. The juices will run clear when the meat is ready.

As the slow cooker heats up it forms a water seal just under the lid. Lifting the lid adds 20 minutes to the cooking time.

• Remove the slow cooker pot from the housing when the food is cooked and then serve. Leftover food should be transferred to a plastic container, covered and allowed to cool at room temperature before being chilled in the refrigerator.

• Never reheat cooked food in a slow cooker. Reheat a cooked casserole in a saucepan on the hob and make sure that you bring it to the boil and cook it through thoroughly. Only reheat cooked food once.

• Never try to repair an electrical fault yourself – contact the manufacturer for advice.

Simply soups

Salmon

This quick and easy soup is flavoured with miso, a Japanese paste made from fermented soya beans. You can also add mirin, a Japanese cooking wine made from rice.

Serves 6

Preparation time: 15 minutes
Cooking time: 1 hour 40 minutes–2 hours 10 minutes
Cooking temperature: low and high
Slow cooker size: standard round or oval

4 salmon steaks, about 125 g (4 oz) each
1 carrot, thinly sliced
4 spring onions, thinly sliced
4 cup mushrooms, about 125 g (4 oz) in total, thinly sliced
1 large red chilli, halved, deseeded and finely chopped
2 cm (¾ inch) fresh root ginger, peeled and finely chopped
3 tablespoons miso
1 tablespoon dark soy sauce
2 tablespoons mirin (optional)
1.2 litres (2 pints) hot fish stock
75 g (3 oz) mangetout, thinly sliced
coriander leaves, to garnish

1 Preheat the slow cooker if necessary – see manufacturer's instructions. Rinse the salmon in cold water, drain and place in the slow cooker pot. Put the carrot, spring onions, mushrooms, chilli and ginger on top of the fish.

2 Add the miso, soy sauce and mirin, if using, to the hot stock and stir until the miso has dissolved. Pour the stock mixture over the salmon and vegetables and cover.

3 Cook on low for 1½–2 hours or until the fish is tender and the soup is piping hot. Lift the fish out with a slotted spoon and transfer it to a plate. Flake it into chunky pieces, discarding the skin and any bones.

4 Return the fish to the slow cooker pot and add the mangetout. Cook on high for 10 minutes or until the mangetout are just tender, then ladle the soup into bowls and serve topped with coriander leaves.

Tip
- **Miso and mirin are available from most larger supermarkets and from specialist oriental stores. Once opened, store miso in the refrigerator.**

in hot miso broth

Crystal hot and sour chicken soup

This colourful Thai-style soup is brimming with oriental flavours. If you prefer, use the same weight of boneless, skinless chicken thighs instead of the chicken breasts.

Serves 6

Preparation time: 20 minutes
Cooking time: 5¼–7¼ hours
Cooking temperature: low and high
Slow cooker size: standard round or oval

1 tablespoon sunflower oil
1 onion, finely chopped
3 boneless, skinless chicken breasts, about 550 g
   (1 lb 2 oz) in total, diced
2 garlic cloves, finely chopped
3 teaspoons red Thai curry paste
1.2 litres (2 pints) chicken stock
2 tablespoons soy sauce
1 tablespoon Thai fish sauce
125 g (4 oz) button mushrooms, sliced
1 large carrot, thinly sliced
125 g (4 oz) mini corn cobs, sliced
50 g (2 oz) mangetout, sliced
coriander or basil leaves, torn into pieces
2 limes, cut into wedges, to serve

1 Preheat the slow cooker if necessary – see manufacturer's instructions. Heat the oil in a large frying pan, add the onion and chicken and fry, stirring, for 5 minutes or until lightly browned. Mix in the garlic and curry paste and cook for 1 minute.

2 Add the stock, soy sauce and fish sauce to the frying pan and bring to the boil. Add the mushrooms and carrot to the slow cooker pot and pour over the hot stock mixture. Cover and cook on low for 5–7 hours or until the chicken is tender.

3 Mix in the corn cobs, mangetout and herbs, cover and cook on high for 15 minutes. Ladle the soup into bowls and serve with lime wedges so that diners can squeeze over lime juice to taste.

Smoked aubergine
with anchovy toasts

Serves 6

Preparation time: 40 minutes
Cooking time: 6–8 hours
Cooking temperature: low
Slow cooker size: standard round or oval

2 large aubergines
2 tablespoons olive oil
1 large onion, chopped
2 garlic cloves, finely chopped
½ teaspoon pimenton (Spanish smoked paprika) or
   chilli powder
500 g (1 lb) plum tomatoes, skinned and chopped
600 ml (1 pint) vegetable or chicken stock
salt and pepper

Anchovy toasts

50 g (2 oz) can anchovy fillets, drained and finely
   chopped
75 g (3 oz) butter, softened
1 small baguette or ½ French stick, sliced

1 Preheat the slow cooker if necessary – see manufacturer's instructions. Prick each aubergine with a fork just below the stalk and cook under a preheated grill for 15 minutes, turning several times, until the skin is blistered and blackened. Transfer to a chopping board and leave to cool.

2 Heat the oil in a large frying pan, add the onion and fry, stirring, for 5 minutes.

3 Cut the aubergines in half and use a spoon to scoop the soft flesh from the skins. Roughly chop the flesh and add it to the onion with the garlic. Fry for 2 minutes, mix in the pimenton or chilli powder and cook for 1 minute. Stir in the tomatoes, stock and salt and pepper and bring to the boil.

4 Transfer the mixture to the slow cooker pot, cover and cook on low for 6–8 hours.

5 Purée the soup until smooth or leave chunky if preferred. Mix the anchovies with the softened butter. Toast the bread lightly and spread with the anchovy butter. Ladle the soup into bowls and float two pieces of toast on each bowl.

Beetroot and carrot

A favourite in eastern European countries, this deep red broth is flavoured with beef stock. Vegetarians could use vegetable stock and add some dried mushrooms for extra flavour.

Serves 6

Preparation time: 25 minutes
Cooking time: 7¼–8¼ hours
Cooking temperature: low and high
Slow cooker size: standard round or oval

25 g (1 oz) butter
1 tablespoon sunflower oil
1 large onion, finely chopped
375 g (12 oz) raw beetroot, trimmed, peeled and
   cut into small dice
2 carrots, cut into small dice
250 g (8 oz) potatoes, cut into small dice
2 garlic cloves, finely chopped
1 litre (1¾ pint) hot beef stock
1 tablespoon tomato purée
2 bay leaves
2 celery sticks, cut into small dice (optional)
125 g (4 oz) red cabbage, finely shredded
salt and pepper

To serve

2 tablespoons red wine vinegar
1 tablespoon caster sugar
300 ml (½ pint) hot beef stock

To garnish

150 ml (¼ pint) double cream
coarsely ground black pepper

1 Preheat the slow cooker if necessary – see manufacturer's instructions. Heat the butter and oil in a large frying pan, add the onion and fry, stirring, for 5 minutes or until softened. Stir in the beetroot, carrots, potatoes and garlic and fry for 2 minutes.

2 Stir in the stock (or as much as you can get in the pan), tomato purée, bay leaves and salt and pepper and bring to the boil, stirring.

3 Put the celery, if using, and red cabbage in the slow cooker pot. Pour over the hot stock mixture (reheat any stock that would not fit into the pan at the beginning and add it to the pot when it is boiling), cover and cook on low for 7–8 hours or until tender.

4 Stir in the vinegar and sugar then purée the soup in batches in a liquidizer or food processor until smooth then return it to the slow cooker. Mix in the extra hot stock and reheat on high for 15 minutes. Ladle the soup into bowls and spoon a little cream over the top of each and sprinkle with a little pepper.

soup with cream

Chunky pistou with Parmesan thins

Serves 6

Preparation time: 25 minutes
Cooking time: 6 hours 15 minutes–8 hours 20 minutes
Cooking temperature: low and high
Slow cooker size: standard round or oval

1 tablespoon olive oil
1 onion, finely chopped
1 baking potato, cut into small dice
1 carrot, cut into small dice
2 garlic cloves, finely chopped
410 g (13¼ oz) can haricot beans, drained
1.2 litres (2 pints) hot chicken or vegetable stock
2 teaspoons pesto, plus extra to serve
100 g (3½ oz) broccoli, cut into small florets,
    stems sliced
100 g (3½ oz) green beans, each cut into 4 slices
2 tomatoes, diced
100 g (3½ oz) Parmesan cheese, coarsely grated
salt and pepper
bunch of basil, to garnish (optional)

1 Preheat the slow cooker if necessary – see manufacturer's instructions. Heat the oil in a large frying pan, add the onion and fry, stirring, for 5 minutes or until lightly browned. Add the potato, carrot and garlic and cook for 2 minutes.

2 Transfer the vegetable mixture to the slow cooker pot, add the haricot beans, hot stock and pesto. Season to taste with salt and pepper, mix thoroughly, cover and cook on low for 6–8 hours.

3 Add the broccoli, green beans and tomatoes, replace the lid and cook on high for 15–20 minutes or until the vegetables are tender.

4 Meanwhile, line a large baking sheet with nonstick baking paper and sprinkle the Parmesan into 18 mounds, leaving space between them for the cheese to spread. Cook in a preheated oven, 190°C, 375°F, Gas Mark 5, for about 5 minutes or until the cheese has melted and is just beginning to brown around the edges. Leave to cool and harden, then peel away the paper.

5 Ladle the soup into bowls, top with extra spoonfuls of pesto, some basil leaves, if liked, and the Parmesan thins.

Lamb hotchpot

This traditional favourite is made with a clear broth speckled with root vegetables and thickened with pearl barley. You can vary the vegetables depending on what's in season, and you could add diced parsnips or turnip.

Serves 6

Preparation time: 20 minutes
Cooking time: 8¼–10¼ hours
Cooking temperature: low and high
Slow cooker size: standard round or oval

15 g (½ oz) butter
1 tablespoon sunflower oil
1 large onion, finely chopped
400 g (13 oz) lamb fillet, diced
175 g (6 oz) carrots, cut into small dice
175 g (6 oz) swedes, cut into small dice
200 g (7 oz) potatoes, cut into small dice
1 leek, thinly sliced (keep white and green
  slices separate)
50 g (2 oz) pearl barley
2–3 sprigs or a little dried rosemary
1.5 litre (2½ pints) lamb stock
salt and pepper
warm bread, to serve

1 Preheat the slow cooker if necessary – see manufacturer's instructions. Heat the butter and oil in a saucepan, add the onion and lamb and cook over a high heat until the lamb is browned and the onion is golden.

2 Stir in the carrots, swedes, potatoes, white sliced leek, pearl barley and rosemary. Add the stock, (or as much as you can get in the pan), season to taste with salt and pepper and bring to the boil.

3 Transfer the mixture to the slow cooker pot, (bring any remaining stock to the boil and add to the pot) cover and cook on low for 8–10 hours or until the pearl barley, vegetables and lamb are tender.

4 Add the green sliced leek tops and cook on high for 15 minutes. Ladle the broth into bowls and serve with warm bread.

Tips

- **This soup freezes well, either in individual sized plastic boxes or plastic bags or in a larger, family-sized container. Microwave or reheat in a saucepan.**

- **For a really filling meal, add small herby dumplings at the same time as the green sliced leeks and cook them for 30 minutes.**

Caldo verde

A favourite Portuguese rustic soup, this is flavoured with diced chorizo sausage and potato. It's almost a meal in itself if it's served with chunks of warm, crusty bread.

Serves 6

Preparation time: 20 minutes
Cooking time: 6 hours 15 minutes–8 hours 20 minutes
Cooking temperature: low and high
Slow cooker size: standard round or oval

2 tablespoons olive oil
2 onions, chopped
2 garlic cloves, finely chopped
150 g (5 oz) chorizo in one piece, skinned and diced
625 g (1¼ lb) or 3 small baking potatoes, cut into
    1 cm (½ inch) dice
1 teaspoon picante pimenton (Spanish hot smoked
    paprika)
1.2 litres (2 pints) hot chicken stock
125 g (4 oz) green cabbage, finely shredded
salt and pepper
warm crusty bread, to serve

1 Preheat the slow cooker if necessary – see manufacturer's instructions. Heat the oil in a large frying pan, add the onions and fry, stirring, for 5 minutes or until lightly browned. Add the garlic, chorizo, potatoes and picante pimenton and cook for 2 minutes.

2 Transfer the mixture to the slow cooker pot, add the hot stock and season to taste with salt and pepper. Cover and cook on low for 6–8 hours.

3 Add the cabbage, replace the lid and cook on high for 15–20 minutes or until the cabbage is tender. Ladle the soup into bowls and serve with warm, crusty bread.

Tip
- **If you are using stock cubes, make up the quantity for this soup with 2 cubes in boiling water. Avoid cubes that are highly seasoned or they will overpower the flavour of the chorizo.**

Smoked gammon

and mixed bean chowder

If you prefer, a small knuckle joint instead of a smoked gammon joint would work equally well in this filling soup.

Serves 6

Preparation time: 20 minutes, plus soaking
Cooking time: 6–7 hours
Cooking temperature: high
Slow cooker size: standard round or oval

500 g (1 lb) boneless smoked gammon joint
150 g (5 oz) country soup mix (blend of dried
    peas, barley, lentils and beans)
2 onions, roughly chopped
1 carrot, diced
1 bay leaf
4 cloves
1.5 litres (2½ pints) vegetable stock
pepper
chopped flat leaf parsley, to garnish
warm crusty bread, to serve

1 Put the gammon joint in a bowl, cover with cold water and transfer to the refrigerator. Put the soup mixture in a separate bowl, cover with cold water and leave at room temperature. Leave both to soak overnight.

2 Preheat the slow cooker if necessary – see manufacturer's instructions. Drain the bean mixture and put it in a saucepan with the onions, carrot, bay leaf, cloves, stock and pepper. Bring to the boil and boil rapidly for 10 minutes, skimming off any scum.

3 Remove the gammon from the soaking water and put it in the slow cooker pot. Top with the bean and stock mixture, cover and cook on high for 6–7 hours or until well cooked.

4 Lift the gammon out of the slow cooker pot, cut away the rind and any fat and break the meat into bite-sized pieces. Return the meat to the slow cooker pot and sprinkle with parsley. Ladle the soup into bowls and serve with warm crusty bread.

Tips

- **If you can't find a small gammon joint, cut off thin slices from a larger piece until the joint will fit into your slow cooker. Grill the slices and serve them with poached eggs and chips for a quick supper or brunch.**

- **If your slow cooker is on the small side, keep back 300 ml (½ pint) stock and add it once you take the gammon joint out at the end.**

- **Warn diners to look out for the cloves.**

Creamy cauliflower with honey cashews

Serves 6

Preparation time: 30 minutes
Cooking time: 4¼–5¼ hours
Cooking temperature: low and high
Slow cooker size: standard round or oval

25 g (1 oz) butter
1 tablespoon olive oil
1 onion, roughly chopped
50 g (2 oz) cashew nuts
750 ml (1¼ pints) vegetable stock
grated nutmeg, to taste
1 large cauliflower, cut into florets and woody core
    discarded
450 ml (¾ pint) full-fat milk
150 ml (¼ pint) double cream
salt and pepper

Caramelized cashew nuts

15 g (½ oz) butter
50 g (2 oz) cashew nuts
1 tablespoon set honey

1 Preheat the slow cooker if necessary – see manufacturer's instructions. Heat the butter and oil in a large frying pan, add the onion and 50 g (2 oz) cashew nuts and fry until just beginning to colour. Add the stock, a little nutmeg and salt and pepper and bring to the boil.

2 Put the cauliflower in the slow cooker pot, add the hot onion mixture, cover and cook on low for 4–5 hours or until the cauliflower is tender.

3 Meanwhile, make the caramelized cashew nuts. Heat the butter in a clean frying pan, add the nuts and cook until they are pale golden. Add the honey and bubble for 1–2 minutes or until the nuts are deep golden and the honey has darkened slightly. Tip on to a baking sheet lined with oiled foil, leave to cool and harden, then break into pieces.

4 Purée the soup in batches in a liquidizer or food processor until smooth. Return it to the slow cooker, stir in the milk and half the cream. Add a little more nutmeg and salt and pepper if wished, then cook on high for 15 minutes or until reheated.

5 Ladle the soup into bowls, swirl the remaining cream over the top and garnish with broken pieces of the caramelized cashew nuts.

Tip
• **If you prefer, use maple syrup to caramelize the cashew nuts.**

Parsnip and apple
soup with chilli and Stilton

Serves 6

Preparation time: 35 minutes
Cooking time: 4¼–5¼ hours
Cooking temperature: low and high
Slow cooker size: standard round or oval

25 g (1 oz) butter
1 tablespoon sunflower oil
1 onion, chopped
625 g (1¼ lb) parsnips, diced
1 cooking apple, about 250 g (8 oz), quartered,
    cored, peeled and diced
1½ teaspoons cumin seeds, crushed
½ teaspoon ground turmeric
900 ml (1½ pints) chicken or vegetable stock
300 ml (½ pint) milk
salt and pepper

Chilli and Stilton butter

75 g (3 oz) Stilton cheese, rind removed
50 g (2 oz) butter
½ teaspoon finely chopped fresh red chilli
2 tablespoons chopped chives (optional)

1 Preheat the slow cooker if necessary – see manufacturer's instructions. Heat the butter and oil in a large frying pan, add the onion and fry, stirring, for 5 minutes until softened but not browned.

2 Add the parsnips, apple, cumin seeds and turmeric and cook for 2 minutes. Add the stock and salt and pepper and bring to the boil. Transfer to the slow cooker pot, cover and cook on low for 4–5 hours or until the parsnips are tender.

3 Meanwhile, make the flavoured butter. Mash the cheese on a plate with the butter. Mix in the chilli and chopped chives, if using. Spoon in a line, about 10 cm (4 inches) long, on a piece of greaseproof paper or foil, cover loosely, then roll backwards and forwards to make a neat cylinder. Twist the ends of the paper or foil to seal, then chill.

4 Purée the soup in batches until smooth. Then return it to the slow cooker. Stir in the milk and cook on high for 15 minutes or until piping hot. Ladle the soup into bowls and top with thin slices of the butter and some long pieces of chive.

Gingered red lentil

This smooth, velvety but spicy soup is flavoured with ginger and cumin and topped with fried onions speckled with fennel, cumin and turmeric, lightly caramelized with a little sugar.

Serves 6

Preparation time: 30 minutes
Cooking time: 6¼–8¼ hours
Cooking temperature: low and high
Slow cooker size: standard round or oval

1 tablespoon olive oil
1 onion, chopped
2 garlic cloves, finely chopped
1 teaspoon fennel seeds, crushed
4 cm (1½ inch) fresh root ginger, peeled and
   finely chopped
900 ml (1½ pints) vegetable or chicken stock
500 g (1 lb) sweet potato, diced
150 g (5 oz) red lentils
300 ml (½ pint) full-fat milk
salt and pepper
warm naan bread, to serve

To garnish

2 tablespoons olive oil
1 onion, thinly sliced
1 teaspoon fennel seeds, crushed
½ teaspoon ground cumin
¼ teaspoon ground turmeric
1 teaspoon caster sugar

1 Preheat the slow cooker if necessary – see manufacturer's instructions. Heat the oil in a large frying pan, add the onion and fry, stirring, for 5 minutes or until lightly browned. Add the garlic, fennel seeds and ginger and cook for 2 minutes.

2 Add the stock and salt and pepper and bring to the boil. Put the sweet potato and lentils in the slow cooker pot, pour over the hot stock mixture, cover and cook on low for 6–8 hours or until the potato and lentils are soft.

3 Purée the soup in batches and return it to the slow cooker. Stir in the milk and cook on high for 15 minutes.

4 Meanwhile, make the garnish. Heat the oil in a clean frying pan, add the onion and fry over a low heat, stirring occasionally, for 10 minutes or until softened. Stir in the spices and sugar, increase the heat slightly and fry for 5 more minutes or until golden brown.

5 Ladle the soup into bowls and sprinkle the spicy onions over the top. Serve with warm naan bread.

Tip
• If you are on a dairy-free diet, add an extra 300 ml (½ pint) of stock instead of the milk at the end of step 3.

and sweet potato soup

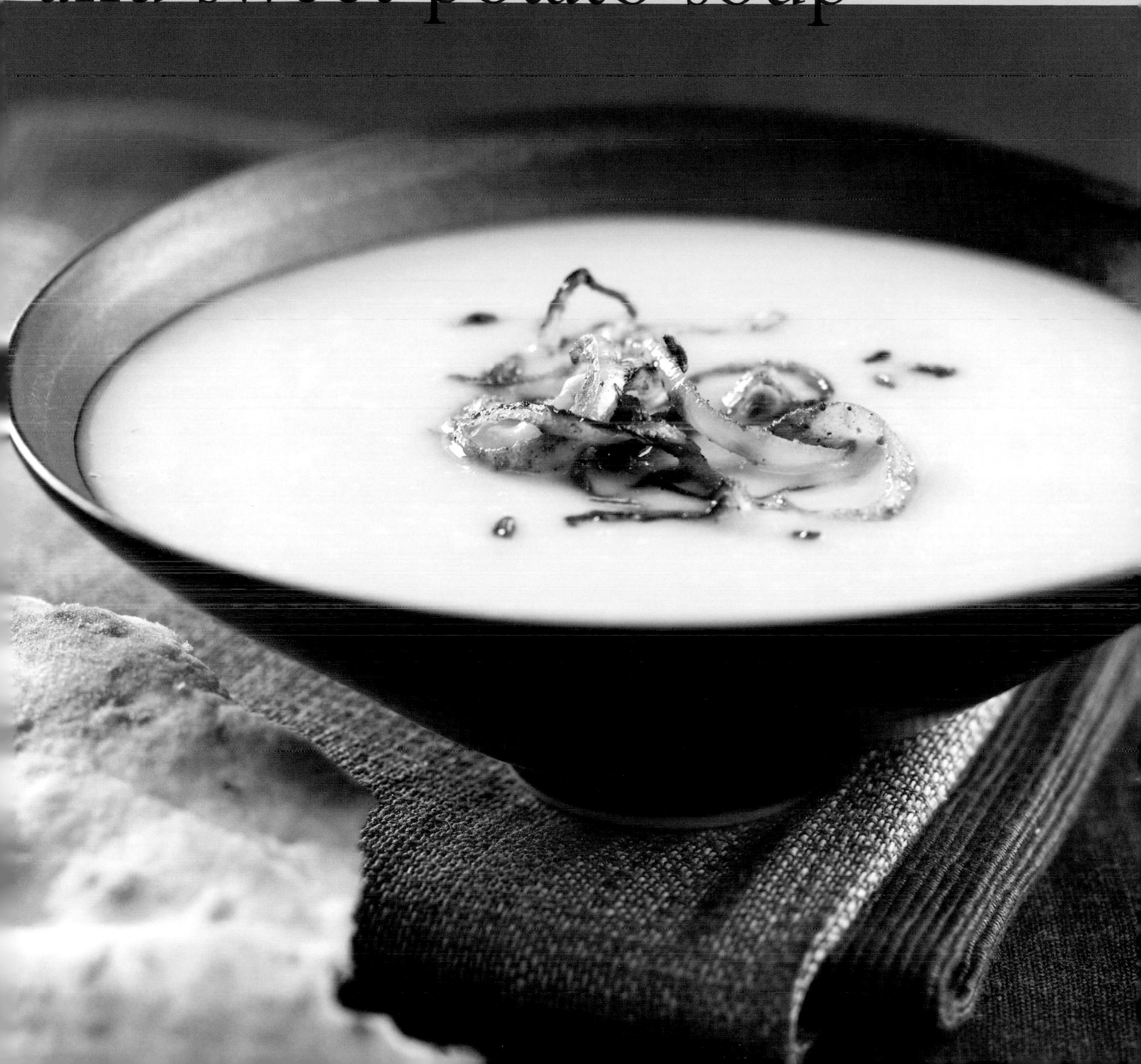

Broad bean, pea and spinach soup

Serves 6

Preparation time: 30 minutes
Cooking time: 4¹/₂–5³/₄ hours
Cooking temperature: low and high
Slow cooker size: standard round or oval

1 tablespoon olive oil
1 onion, chopped
1 baking potato, about 250 g (8 oz), diced
375 g (12 oz) frozen broad beans
900 ml (1¹/₂ pints) chicken or vegetable stock
125 g (4 oz) frozen peas
100 g (3¹/₂ oz) spinach
300 ml (¹/₂ pint) full-fat milk
grated nutmeg
salt and pepper

To garnish

1 tablespoon olive oil
100 g (3¹/₂ oz) pancetta or chorizo sausage, diced
6 tablespoons double cream

1 Preheat the slow cooker if necessary – see manufacturer's instructions. Heat the oil in a large frying pan, add the onion and fry, stirring, for 5 minutes or until lightly browned. Add the potato, beans, stock and salt and pepper and bring to the boil.

2 Transfer the mixture to the slow cooker pot, cover and cook on low for 4–5 hours. Add the peas and spinach, cover and cook on high for 15–30 minutes.

3 Purée the soup in batches and return to the slow cooker. Stir in the milk, add nutmeg to taste, replace the lid and cook on high for 15 minutes or until piping hot.

4 Heat the oil in a clean frying pan and fry the pancetta or chorizo until lightly browned. Ladle the soup into bowls, swirl the cream over the top and sprinkle with the fried pancetta or chorizo.

Tip
• **Try adding 3 tablespoons of chopped mint to this soup just before serving.**

Bloody Mary soup
with chilli oil

Packed with all the flavours of a chilled Bloody Mary cocktail, this smooth soup is the perfect pick-me-up or an excellent starter for a smart dinner party.

Serves 6

Preparation time: 25 minutes
Cooking time: 5–6 hours
Cooking temperature: low
Slow cooker size: standard round or oval

1 tablespoon olive oil
1 onion, chopped
1 red pepper, cored, deseeded and diced
2 celery sticks, sliced
500 g (1 lb) plum tomatoes, chopped
¼ teaspoon chilli powder
600 ml (1 pint) vegetable stock
4 teaspoons Worcestershire sauce
4 teaspoons tomato purée
2 teaspoons caster sugar
4 tablespoons vodka
salt and pepper
warm ciabatta bread, to serve

To garnish
2 tomatoes, sliced
a few celery leaves
chilli-flavoured olive oil

1 Preheat the slow cooker if necessary – see manufacturer's instructions. Heat the oil in a large frying pan, add the onion and fry, stirring, for 5 minutes or until lightly browned.

2 Stir in the red pepper, celery, tomatoes and chilli powder and cook for 2 minutes. Mix in the stock, Worcestershire sauce, tomato purée, sugar and salt and pepper and bring to the boil.

3 Transfer the mixture to the slow cooker pot, cover and cook on low for 5–6 hours. Purée it until smooth in a liquidizer or food processor, then return to the slow cooker. Stir in the vodka, cover and keep hot until required.

4 Ladle the soup into bowls and top each with a tomato slice and a small celery leaf. Drizzle chilli-flavoured oil around the tomato. Serve with warm ciabatta bread.

Delectable
dinners

Pesto baked salmon

The gentle cooking in a slow cooker means that the fish stays moist and there is no danger that it will break up. Serve with rice mixed with lots of chopped basil and parsley or with baby new potatoes.

Serves 4
Preparation time: 20 minutes
Cooking time: 3–3½ hours
Cooking temperature: low
Slow cooker size: standard oval

500 g (1 lb) salmon fillet, cut from the thick end
  of the fillet
2 teaspoons pesto
1 red pepper, cored, deseeded and chopped
250 g (8 oz) cherry tomatoes, halved
4 spring onions, thinly sliced
200 ml (7 fl oz) dry white wine
150 ml (¼ pint) fish stock
salt and pepper
basil leaves, to garnish

1 Preheat the slow cooker if necessary – see manufacturer's instructions. Take a long piece of foil and fold it in half widthways. Place the salmon on the centre of the foil and spread the top with the pesto.

2 Holding the ends of the foil, lower the salmon into the slow cooker pot (see page 11). Add the red pepper, tomatoes and spring onions. Pour the wine and stock into a frying pan, season to taste with salt and pepper and bring to the boil. Pour the liquid into the slow cooker. Fold the ends of the foil down if necessary so that they fit inside the slow cooker, then cover and cook on low for 3–3½ hours or until the fish flakes into opaque pieces and the vegetables are just tender.

3 Spoon the vegetables on to plates. Use the foil strap to lift the salmon from the pot and cut it into 4 pieces. Arrange these next to the vegetables. Pour the stock into a frying pan and boil rapidly for 2–3 minutes or until it is reduced by half. Pour the sauce over the salmon and serve garnished with basil leaves.

Squid in puttanesca sauce

The squid takes on the full flavour of the rich Italian tomato, caper and olive sauce and almost melts in the mouth. Serve tossed with cooked linguine or another pasta of your choice and a glass of robust red wine.

Serves 4

Preparation time: 25 minutes
Cooking time: 3½–4½ hours
Cooking temperature: low
Slow cooker size: standard round or oval

500 g (1 lb) prepared squid tubes
1 tablespoon olive oil
1 onion, chopped
2 garlic cloves, finely chopped
400 g (13 oz) can chopped tomatoes
150 ml (¼ pint) fish stock
4 teaspoons capers, drained
50 g (2 oz) pitted black olives
2–3 sprigs of thyme, plus extra to garnish (optional)
1 teaspoon fennel seeds, roughly crushed
1 teaspoon caster sugar
salt and pepper
linguine, to serve

1 Preheat the slow cooker if necessary – see manufacturer's instructions. Take the tentacles out of the squid tubes and rinse inside the tubes with cold water. Put them in a sieve and rinse the outside of the tubes and the tentacles. Drain well, put the tentacles in a small bowl, cover and return to the refrigerator. Thickly slice the squid tubes.

2 Heat the oil in a large frying pan, add the onion and fry, stirring, for 5 minutes or until golden. Add the garlic and cook for 2 minutes. Stir in the tomatoes, stock, capers, olives, thyme, fennel seeds, sugar and salt and pepper and bring to the boil.

3 Transfer the sauce to the slow cooker pot, add the sliced squid and press the pieces below the surface of the sauce. Cover and cook on low for 3–4 hours.

4 Stir the squid mixture and add the squid tentacles, pressing them below the surface of the sauce. Cook on low for 30 minutes. Serve tossed with cooked linguine, and thyme sprigs, if using.

Bobotie

This spiced meatloaf is a South African dish, which can be eaten hot with spiced rice or cold with tomato salad.

Serves 4–5

Preparation time: 30 minutes
Cooking time: 5½–6½ hours
Cooking temperature: high
Slow cooker size: standard oval

1 tablespoon sunflower oil
500 g (1 lb) lean minced beef
1 onion, finely chopped
2 garlic cloves, finely chopped
4 teaspoons curry paste
1 tablespoon red or white wine vinegar
1 tablespoon tomato purée
50 g (2 oz) sultanas
1 banana, chopped
50 g (2 oz) fresh white breadcrumbs
3 small bay leaves
salt and pepper

Topping

2 eggs
large pinch ground turmeric
4 tablespoons milk

1 Preheat the slow cooker if necessary – see manufacturer's instructions. Heat the oil in a large frying pan, add the mince and onion and fry over a high heat, stirring, until the mince is evenly browned.

2 Add the garlic, curry paste, vinegar and tomato purée, then the sultanas, chopped banana and breadcrumbs to the pan and season with salt and pepper.

3 Spoon the mixture into a lightly oiled soufflé dish or ovenproof dish, 13 cm (5 inches) across and 9 cm (3 inches) high, and press it into an even layer. Press the bay leaves on top and cover with foil.

4 Use foil straps or a string handle to lower the dish into the slow cooker pot (see page 13). Pour boiling water into the pot so that it come halfway up the sides of the dish. Cover and cook on high for 5–6 hours or until the meatloaf is cooked all the way through.

5 Make the topping. Beat together the eggs, turmeric, milk and salt and pepper and pour the mixture over the bay leaves. Cover loosely with foil and cook on high for 30 minutes on hot or until set. Carefully lift the dish out of the slow cooker pot and serve warm or cold.

Thi bo kho

This Vietnamese beef stew is flavoured with yellow bean paste and five spice powder. Serve it with rice or fried noodles for a tasty midweek supper.

Serves 4

Preparation time: 30 minutes
Cooking time: 8–10 hours
Cooking temperature: low
Slow cooker size: standard round or oval

1 tablespoon sunflower oil
250 g (8 oz) shallots, halved
750 g (1½ lb) braising beef, cubed
2 garlic cloves, finely chopped
2 tablespoons plain flour
450 ml (¾ pint) beef stock
3 tablespoons yellow bean paste
grated rind of 1 lemon, plus extra rind to garnish
1 teaspoon five spice powder
salt and pepper
100 g (3½ oz) well-rinsed bean sprouts, to garnish
rice or fried noodles, to serve

1 Preheat the slow cooker if necessary – see manufacturer's instructions. Heat the oil in a large frying pan, add the shallots and fry for 5 minutes or until golden. Remove them from the pan with a slotted spoon and transfer to a plate.

2 Add the beef to the pan, a few pieces at a time, until all the meat has been added, then cook over a high heat, stirring until evenly browned. Add the garlic and cook for 2 minutes.

3 Stir in the flour, then gradually mix in the stock. Add the yellow bean paste, lemon rind, five spice powder and season with salt and pepper. Bring to the boil, stirring.

4 Spoon the beef mixture into the slow cooker pot, add the shallots and press the meat below the surface of the liquid. Cover and cook on low for 8–10 hours or until the meat is tender.

5 Garnish the casserole with stir-fried bean sprouts and extra lemon rind and serve with rice or fried noodles.

Tip

- **If you use stock cubes, choose one with a mild flavour so that it does not overpower the yellow bean paste.**

Olive and lemon meatballs

Buying a pack of mince in the weekly supermarket dash needn't mean Spaghetti Bolognese again. Here the mince is flavoured with black olives and lemon rind, shaped into meatballs and gently simmered with a rich tomato sauce.

Serves 4

Preparation time: 30 minutes
Cooking time: 6–8 hours
Cooking temperature: low
Slow cooker size: standard round or oval

Meatballs
50 g (2 oz) pitted black olives, chopped
grated rind of ½ lemon
500 g (1 lb) extra lean minced beef
1 egg yolk
salt and pepper

Sauce
1 tablespoon olive oil
1 onion, chopped
2 garlic cloves, finely chopped
400 g (13 oz) can chopped tomatoes
1 teaspoon caster sugar
150 ml (¼ pint) chicken stock

To garnish
grated rind of 1 lemon
small basil leaves

1 Preheat the slow cooker if necessary – see manufacturer's instructions. Make the meatballs. Put all the ingredients in a bowl and mix with a wooden spoon. Wet your hands and shape the mixture into 20 balls.

2 Heat the oil in a large frying pan, add the meatballs and cook over a high heat, turning until browned on all sides. Lift them out of pan with a slotted spoon and transfer to a plate.

3 Make the sauce. Add the onion to the pan and fry, stirring, for 5 minutes or until lightly browned. Add the garlic, tomatoes, sugar, stock and salt and pepper and bring to the boil, stirring.

4 Transfer the meatballs to the slow cooker pot, pour over the hot sauce, cover and cook on low for 6–8 hours. Sprinkle with lemon rind and basil leaves to garnish. Serve with tagliatelle tossed with chopped basil and melted butter.

with tomato sauce

Gingered beef

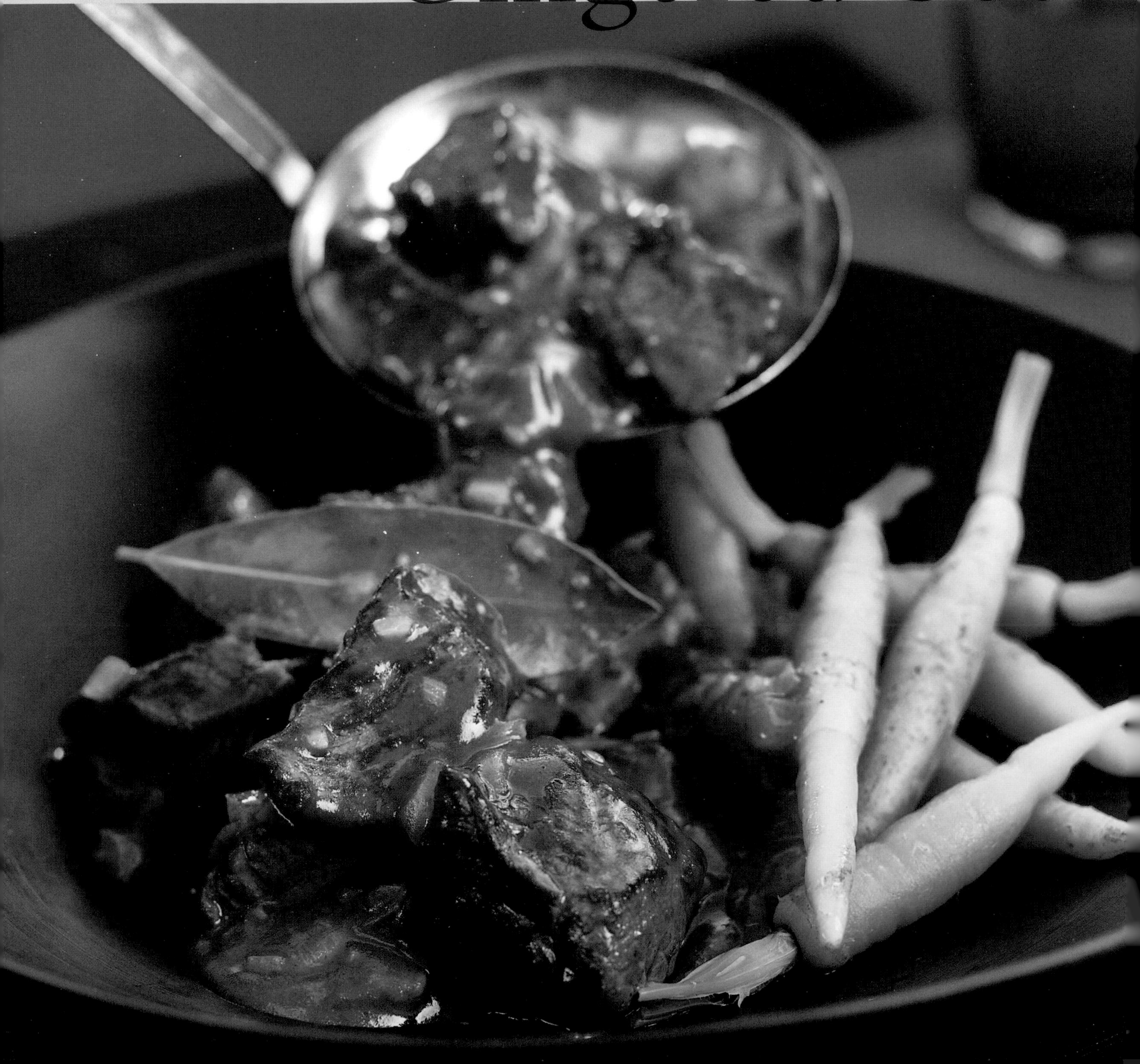

with bay

Bay leaves have been popular in meaty stews since Roman times, and here they are combined with root ginger for a rustic-style casserole that is delicious served with mashed potato or celeriac.

Serves 4

Preparation time: 20 minutes
Cooking time: 8–10 hours
Cooking temperature: low
Slow cooker size: standard round or oval

2 tablespoons olive oil
750 g (1½ lb) lean braising beef, cubed
1 onion, chopped
2 tablespoons plain flour
450 ml (¾ pint) beef stock
1 tablespoon tomato purée
1 tablespoon balsamic vinegar
2 teaspoons dark muscovado sugar
3 bay leaves
4 cm (1½ inch) fresh root ginger, peeled and finely chopped
salt and pepper
baby carrots, to serve

1 Preheat the slow cooker if necessary – see manufacturer's instructions. Heat the oil in a large frying pan, add the beef, a few pieces at a time, until all the meat has been added, then fry over a high heat, stirring, until evenly browned. Lift out of the pan with a slotted spoon and transfer to a plate.

2 Add the onion to the pan and fry, stirring, for 5 minutes or until softened and lightly browned. Stir in the flour, then mix in the stock, tomato purée, vinegar, sugar, bay leaves and ginger. Season with salt and pepper and bring to the boil.

3 Transfer the beef to the slow cooker pot, pour over the hot stock, cover and cook on low for 8–10 hours. Serve with steamed baby carrots tossed with a little butter.

Tip
- **This casserole would also be delicious with dumplings. Shape and add the dumplings 30–45 minutes before the end of cooking and increase the temperature from low to high.**

Beef adobo

This recipe, flavoured with soy sauce and vinegar, is traditionally eaten in the Philippines, but it's also a popular dish in Spain and Gibraltar.

Serves 4

Preparation time: 25 minutes
Cooking time: 8–10 hours
Cooking temperature: low
Slow cooker size: standard round or oval

1 tablespoon sunflower oil
750 g (1½ lb) braising beef (fat removed), cubed
1 large onion, sliced
2 garlic cloves, finely chopped
2 tablespoons plain flour
450 ml (¾ pint) beef stock
4 tablespoons soy sauce
4 tablespoons rice or wine vinegar
1 tablespoon caster sugar
2 bay leaves
juice of 1 lime
salt and pepper
rice, to serve

To garnish

1 carrot, cut into thin sticks
½ bunch of spring onions, cut into shreds
coriander leaves

1 Preheat the slow cooker if necessary – see manufacturer's instructions. Heat the oil in a large frying pan and add the beef, a few pieces at a time, until all the meat has been added. Fry over a high heat, turning until evenly browned, lift out of the pan with a slotted spoon and transfer to a plate.

2 Add the onion to the pan and fry for 5 minutes or until it is just beginning to brown. Mix in the garlic and cook for 2 minutes. Stir in the flour, then gradually mix in the stock. Add the soy sauce, vinegar, sugar, bay leaves and salt and pepper and bring to the boil, stirring.

3 Transfer the beef to the slow cooker pot, pour over the onion and stock mixture, cover and cook on low for 8–10 hours.

4 Stir in lime juice to taste. Serve in shallow bowls lined with rice and garnish with carrot sticks, shredded spring onion and coriander leaves.

Abruzzi lamb

The foothills of the Abruzzi, a mountainous region in central Italy, are famous for lamb dishes, especially those slowly cooked with garlic, olive oil and tomatoes.

Serves 4–5

Preparation time: 30 minutes
Cooking time: 8–10 hours
Cooking temperature: low
Slow cooker size: standard round or oval

1 tablespoon olive oil
750 g (1½ lb) lean lamb, leg or chump steaks, cubed
75 g (3 oz) pancetta, diced
1 large onion, chopped
2 garlic cloves, finely chopped
2 tablespoons plain flour
300 ml (½ pint) lamb or chicken stock
1 tablespoon tomato purée
2 teaspoons light muscovado sugar
2–3 sprigs of rosemary
250 g (8 oz) cherry tomatoes
salt and pepper

To serve
rigatoni or pappardelle
green salad

1 Preheat the slow cooker if necessary – see manufacturer's instructions. Heat the oil in a large frying pan and add the lamb, a few pieces at a time, until all the meat has been added. Fry over a high heat, stirring until evenly browned, then lift the lamb out of the pan with a slotted spoon and transfer to a plate.

2 Add the pancetta and onion to the pan and fry, stirring, for 5 minutes or until lightly browned. Add the garlic and cook for 2 minutes. Stir in the flour, then mix in the stock. Add the tomato purée, sugar, rosemary and salt and pepper and bring to the boil, stirring.

3 Spoon the meat and any juices into the slow cooker pot, pour the hot onion mixture over the top, then add the whole tomatoes. Cover with the lid, then cook on low for 8–10 hours or until the lamb is tender.

4 Serve the lamb spooned over cooked pasta such as pappardelle or rigatoni and accompanied with a salad.

Tips

- **If you like, replace 150 ml (¼ pint) stock with the same quantity of red wine.**

- **If you do not have any fresh rosemary, use a small amount of dried rosemary.**

Kleftico-style lamb

This moist half shoulder of lamb is flavoured with wine, lemon and honey and is so tender that it practically falls off the bone as you serve it. Serve with plain boiled potatoes or rice mixed with chopped parsley and toasted pine nuts.

Serves 4

Preparation time: 25 minutes
Cooking time: 7–8 hours
Cooking temperature: high
Slow cooker size: standard oval

½ shoulder of lamb, 900 g–1 kg (1 lb 14 oz–2 lb)
2 garlic cloves, sliced
1 tablespoon olive oil
2 large onions, halved and thinly sliced
2 tablespoons plain flour
300 ml (½ pint) lamb stock
150 ml (¼ pint) white wine or extra stock
½ lemon, thinly sliced
1 tablespoon set or clear honey
4–5 sprigs of rosemary, plus extra to garnish
50 g (2 oz) stoned dates, halved
40 g (1½ oz) raisins
salt and pepper

1 Preheat the slow cooker if necessary – see manufacturer's instructions. Make small slits at intervals over the top of the lamb down through the fat and into the meat and insert a small slice of garlic into each slit.

2 Heat the oil in a large frying pan and fry the lamb over a high heat until browned all over. Lift the lamb out of the pan and transfer it to a plate. Add the onions and fry, stirring, for 5 minutes or until lightly browned. Stir in the flour, then mix in the stock, wine, if using, lemon slices and honey. Season with salt and pepper and bring to the boil.

3 Put 2 rosemary stems in the base of the slow cooker, add the lamb, the remaining rosemary, the dates and raisins, then pour over the hot stock mixture. Cover and cook on high for 7–8 hours. Serve in shallow bowls, garnished with rosemary.

Tips

- **This recipe is best suited to an oval slow cooker. Check that the lamb will fit in your slow cooker before you begin.**

- **The lamb will simply fall off the bone when it's cooked, so don't try to carve it into neat slices.**

Spiced pork chops with sweet potato

A sweet and sour mix of cubed sweet potato, diced cooking apple and pork chops, gently simmered with an aromatic blend of allspice, cinnamon and chilli.

Serves 4

Preparation time: 30 minutes
Cooking time: 7–8 hours
Cooking temperature: high
Slow cooker size: standard round or oval

1 tablespoon olive oil
4 pork shoulder steaks or boneless spare rib chops,
    about 700 g (1 lb 7 oz) in total
1 onion, chopped
2 garlic cloves, finely chopped
2 tablespoons plain flour
450 ml (¾ pint) chicken stock
400 g (13 oz) can chopped tomatoes
½ teaspoon ground allspice
½ teaspoon ground cinnamon
1 large dried chilli (optional)
1 cooking apple, about 250 g (8 oz), cored, peeled
    and diced
2 large sweet potatoes, about 700 g (1 lb 7 oz)
    in total, cut into 2.5 cm (1 inch) cubes
salt and pepper

1 Preheat the slow cooker if necessary – see manufacturer's instructions. Heat the oil in a large frying pan, add the pork and fry over a high heat until browned on both sides. Lift it out with a slotted spoon and transfer to a plate.

2 Add the onion to the pan and fry, stirring, for 5 minutes or until lightly browned. Mix in the garlic, then the flour. Gradually stir in the stock and tomatoes, then the spices and chilli, if using, and season to taste with salt and pepper. Bring to the boil.

3 Put the pork in the slow cooker pot, add the apple and sweet potatoes and pour over the sauce. Cover and cook on high for 7–8 hours. Spoon into bowls and serve with warmed bread.

Tip

- **Although there may seem to be a lot of sauce at the end, it is vital so that the potatoes cook evenly. Serve with spoons and lots of bread to mop it up.**

Pork, orange & star anise

This is a great everyday casserole with a hint of oriental spice and mellow-tasting plum sauce. It's delicious served on a bed of parsnip mash.

Serves 4

Preparation time: 20 minutes
Cooking time: 8–10 hours
Cooking temperature: low
Slow cooker size: standard round or oval

1 tablespoon sunflower oil
4 pork shoulder steaks or boneless spare rib chops, about 700 g (1 lb 7 oz) in total, each cut into 3
1 onion, chopped
2 tablespoons plain flour
450 ml (¾ pint) chicken stock
grated rind and juice of 1 orange
3 tablespoons plum sauce
2 tablespoons soy sauce
3–4 whole star anise
1 fresh or dried red chilli, halved (optional)
salt and pepper
grated orange rind, to garnish

To serve

mashed potatoes mixed with steamed green vegetables, such as peas and cabbage

1 Preheat the slow cooker if necessary – see manufacturer's instructions. Heat the oil in a large frying pan, add the pieces of pork and fry over a high heat until browned on both sides. Lift the pork out of the pan with a slotted spoon and transfer to a plate.

2 Add the onion to the pan and fry, stirring, for 5 minutes or until lightly browned. Stir in the flour, then mix in the stock, orange rind and juice, plum sauce, soy sauce, star anise and chilli, if using. Season with salt and pepper and bring to the boil, stirring.

3 Transfer the pork to the slow cooker pot and pour the sauce over it. Cover and cook on low for 8–10 hours. Serve with mashed potatoes mixed with steamed green vegetables and garnish with grated orange rind.

Tips

• **Warn diners not to eat the star anise.**

• **If you like garlic, add 2 cloves, finely chopped, just after frying the onions.**

• **If you don't have any star anise, use a cinnamon stick, broken in half.**

Lemon chicken

Whole chicken breasts are gently simmered with garlic and lemon wedges and finished with pak choi, sugar snap peas and minted crème fraîche. They're delicious served with a couscous salad.

Serves 4

Preparation time: 20 minutes
Cooking time: 3¼–4¼ hours
Cooking temperature: high
Slow cooker size: standard round or oval

1 tablespoon olive oil
4 boneless, skinless chicken breasts, about 550 g
   (1 lb 2 oz) in total
1 onion, chopped
2 garlic cloves, finely chopped
2 tablespoons plain flour
450 ml (¾ pint) chicken stock
½ lemon (cut in half lengthways), cut into 4 wedges
2 pak choi, thickly sliced
125 g (4 oz) sugar snap peas, halved lengthways
4 tablespoons crème fraîche
2 tablespoons chopped mint and parsley mixed
salt and pepper
couscous salad, to serve

1 Preheat the slow cooker if necessary – see manufacturer's instructions. Heat the oil in a large frying pan, add the chicken breasts and fry over a high heat until browned on both sides. Remove from the pan and transfer to a plate. Add the onion to the pan and fry, stirring, for 5 minutes or until lightly browned.

2 Stir in the garlic and flour, then mix in the stock and lemon wedges. Season with salt and pepper and bring to the boil.

3 Put the chicken breasts in the slow cooker pot, pour the hot stock mixture over them and press the chicken below the surface of the liquid. Cover and cook on high for 3–4 hours.

4 Add the pak choi and sugar snap peas and cook on high for 15 minutes or until just tender. Lift out the chicken, slice the pieces and arrange them on plates. Stir the crème fraîche and herbs into the sauce, then spoon it and the vegetables over the chicken. Serve with couscous mixed with finely chopped tomato, red onion and red pepper.

Kashmiri butter chicken

This mild, delicately fragrant curry has a rich creamy sauce that will please all your guests, no matter what their preferences. Serve it with plain boiled rice or warm naan bread.

Serves 4

Preparation time: 30 minutes
Cooking time: 5–7 hours
Cooking temperature: low
Slow cooker size: standard round or oval

2 onions, quartered
3 garlic cloves
4 cm (1½ inch) fresh root ginger, peeled
1 large red chilli, halved, seeds discarded
8 boneless, skinless chicken thighs
1 tablespoon sunflower oil
25 g (1 oz) butter
1 teaspoon cumin seeds, crushed
1 teaspoon fennel seeds, crushed
4 cardamom pods, crushed
1 teaspoon paprika
1 teaspoon ground turmeric
¼ teaspoon ground cinnamon
300 ml (½ pint) chicken stock
1 tablespoon light muscovado sugar
2 tablespoons tomato purée
5 tablespoons double cream
salt

To garnish
2 tablespoons flaked almonds, toasted
sprigs of coriander

1 Preheat the slow cooker if necessary – see manufacturer's instructions. Blend the onions, garlic, ginger and chilli in a food processor or liquidizer or chop finely.

2 Cut each chicken thigh into 4 pieces. Heat the oil in a large frying pan and add the chicken, a few pieces at a time, until all the meat has been added. Cook over a high heat until evenly browned. Lift the chicken pieces out of the pan with a slotted spoon and transfer to a plate.

3 Add the butter to the frying pan and when it has melted add the onion paste. Cook over a more moderate heat until it is just beginning to colour. Stir in the crushed seeds, cardamom seeds and pods and ground spices. Cook for 1 minute, then mix in the stock, sugar, tomato purée and salt. Bring to the boil, stirring.

4 Transfer the chicken to the slow cooker pot, pour the onion mixture and sauce over the top and press the pieces of chicken below the surface of the liquid. Cover and cook on low for 5–7 hours.

5 Stir in the cream and serve garnished with toasted flaked almonds and sprigs of coriander.

Frikadeller

These Danish meatballs, which are cooked in a deep yellow mustard sauce, can be made with minced pork instead of turkey. Serve them in shallow bowls with creamy mashed potatoes or celeriac, a side dish of diced dill cucumbers and a spoon to scoop up the delicious sauce.

Serves 4

Preparation time: 30 minutes
Cooking time: 6–8 hours
Cooking temperature: low
Slow cooker size: standard round or oval

Meatballs

1 onion, finely chopped
500 g (1 lb) minced turkey
50 g (2 oz) fresh white breadcrumbs
1 egg yolk
1 tablespoon sunflower oil
salt and pepper
mashed potatoes, to serve
sprigs of flat leaf parsley, to garnish

Sauce

50 g (2 oz) butter
1 onion, finely chopped
40 g (1½ oz) plain flour
600 ml (1 pint) chicken stock
3 teaspoons mild Swedish or Dijon mustard
½ teaspoon ground turmeric

1 Preheat the slow cooker if necessary – see manufacturer's instructions. Make the meatballs. Mix together the onion, turkey, breadcrumbs, egg yolk and plenty of salt and pepper in a mixing bowl. Wet your hands and shape the mixture into 20 small meatballs.

2 Heat the oil in a large frying pan, add the meatballs and cook over a high heat, turning until evenly browned. Lift them out with a slotted spoon and transfer to a plate.

3 Make the sauce. Melt the butter in a clean frying pan, add the onion and fry gently for 5 minutes or until softened. Stir in the flour, then gradually mix in the stock and bring to the boil, stirring until smooth. Stir in the mustard and turmeric and season with salt and pepper.

4 Transfer the meatballs to the slow cooker pot, pour the sauce over them, then cover and cook on low for 6–8 hours. Serve with mashed potatoes and garnish with flat leaf parsley.

Tamarind chilli chicken

This spicy recipe mixes the sweet, pungent pulp from tamarind pods with chilli, garlic, brown sugar and ground turmeric to create a deliciously mellow dish.

Serves 4

Preparation time: 30 minutes
Cooking time: 8–10 hours
Cooking temperature: low
Slow cooker size: standard round or oval

8 boneless, skinless chicken thighs, about 1 kg (2 lb)
  in total
1 tablespoon sunflower oil
1 onion, chopped
1 red pepper, cored, deseeded and chopped
1 red chilli, halved, cored and chopped (seeds
  optional)
2 garlic cloves, finely chopped
1 tablespoon tamarind paste
1 tablespoon dark brown sugar
1 teaspoon ground turmeric
2 tablespoons plain flour
450 ml (¾ pint) chicken stock
salt and pepper
sprigs of coriander, to garnish
boiled rice, to serve

1 Preheat the slow cooker if necessary – see manufacturer's instructions. Cut the chicken thighs into chunks. Heat the oil in a large frying pan and add the chicken, a few pieces at a time, until all the meat is in the pan. Fry over a high heat until it is just beginning to brown. Transfer to a plate.

2 Add the onion to the pan and fry until lightly browned. Stir in the red pepper, chilli and garlic and cook for 2 minutes. Mix in the tamarind, sugar and turmeric and cook for a further minute. Mix in the flour, then gradually add the stock, season to taste with salt and pepper and bring to the boil.

3 Put the chicken in the slow cooker pot, pour over the onion and stock mixture, cover and cook on low for 8–10 hours. Serve in small bowls, garnished with coriander sprigs and accompanied by boiled rice.

Tip

- **Chillies vary tremendously in heat. The larger, fatter red chillies have been used here, and if you would like a little extra heat add the seeds. If you like very spicy foods, use a thin Thai red chilli or rounded Scotch Bonnet chilli.**

Peppered lentils
with chermoula

This lentil dish is just as delicious served cold as a salad or as a filling with rocket leaves for pitta bread as it is hot with griddled pittas. You might also like to try it spooned over baked potatoes.

Serves 4

Preparation time: 30 minutes
Cooking time: 7–9 hours
Cooking temperature: low
Slow cooker size: standard round or oval

1 tablespoon olive oil
1 large onion, roughly chopped
3 peppers (red, orange and yellow), cored, deseeded
  and chopped
2 garlic cloves, finely chopped
400 g (13 oz) can chopped tomatoes
300 ml (½ pint) vegetable stock
1 tablespoon tomato purée
1 dried or fresh red chilli, halved
150 g (5 oz) Puy lentils
salt and pepper
griddled pitta breads, to serve

Chermoula

2 tablespoons chopped coriander or parsley
2 garlic cloves, finely chopped
½ teaspoon cumin seeds, roughly crushed
½ teaspoon coriander seeds, roughly crushed
grated rind and juice of 1 lime

1 Preheat the slow cooker if necessary – see manufacturer's instructions. Heat the oil in a large frying pan, add the onion and fry for 5 minutes or until lightly browned.

2 Stir in the peppers and garlic and fry for 2 minutes. Mix in the tomatoes, stock, tomato purée, chilli and salt and pepper and bring to the boil.

3 Add the lentils to the slow cooker pot, pour in the pepper and tomato mixture so that the lentils are covered. Cover and cook on low for 7–9 hours or until the lentils are tender.

4 Make the chermoula. Put all the ingredients in a small bowl and mix together. Spoon the lentil mixture into shallow bowls, top with spoonfuls of chermoula and serve with griddled pitta breads.

Dum aloo

For a healthy, meat-free supper serve this spiced new potato and spinach curry with a lentil dhal and plain rice or hot naan bread.

Serves 4

Preparation time: 15 minutes
Cooking time: 6¼–7¼ hours
Cooking temperature: high
Slow cooker size: standard round or oval

2 tablespoons sunflower oil
1 large onion, sliced
1 teaspoon cumin seeds, crushed
4 cardamom pods, crushed
1 teaspoon black onion seeds (optional)
1 teaspoon ground turmeric
½ teaspoon ground cinnamon
2.5 cm (1 inch) fresh root ginger, peeled and finely
   chopped
400 g (13 oz) can chopped tomatoes
300 ml (½ pint) vegetable stock
1 teaspoon caster sugar
750 g (1½ lb) baby new potatoes
100 g (3½ oz) baby leaf spinach
salt and pepper
coriander leaves, to garnish

1 Preheat the slow cooker if necessary – see manufacturer's instructions. Heat the oil in a large frying pan, add the onion and fry, stirring, for 5 minutes or until lightly browned.

2 Mix in the cumin seeds, cardamom pods and seeds, onion seeds, if using, ground spices and ginger. Cook for 1 minute, then mix in the tomatoes, stock, sugar and season with salt and pepper. Bring to the boil, stirring.

3 Cut the potatoes into thick slices or halves (if they are small) so that all the pieces are of a similar size. Transfer to the slow cooker pot and pour the sauce over the top.

4 Cover and cook on high for 6–7 hours or until the potatoes are tender. Add the spinach and cook on high for 15 minutes more until it is just wilted. Stir the curry and serve sprinkled with torn coriander leaves.

Tip
• **If you like curries on the hot side, add a fresh chopped red chilli or some dried chilli powder at step 2.**

Red Thai pumpkin curry

Cubes of golden butternut squash, baby new potatoes and carrots are simmered in a creamy coconut milk sauce lightly spiced with Thai curry paste, garlic and soy sauce.

Serves 4

Preparation time: 25 minutes
Cooking time: 7–8 hours
Cooking temperature: low and high
Slow cooker size: standard round or oval

1 tablespoon sunflower oil
1 onion, chopped
4 teaspoons red Thai curry paste
2 garlic cloves, finely chopped
400 ml (14 fl oz) can reduced-fat coconut milk
300 ml (½ pint) vegetable stock
1 tablespoon Thai fish sauce (optional)
1 tablespoon soy sauce
1 butternut squash, about 700 g (1 lb 7 oz), peeled, deseeded and cut into chunks
250 g (8 oz) baby new potatoes, thickly sliced
250 g (8 oz) carrots, thinly sliced
sprigs of coriander or basil (optional)
125 g (4 oz) medium rice noodles

1 Preheat the slow cooker if necessary – see manufacturer's instructions. Heat the oil in a large frying pan, add the onion and fry, stirring, for 5 minutes or until lightly browned. Mix in the curry paste and garlic and cook for 1 minute. Stir in the coconut milk, stock, fish sauce, if using, and soy sauce. Bring to the boil, stirring.

2 Put the butternut squash, potatoes and carrots into the slow cooker pot. Pour over the sauce, press the vegetables down into the liquid, cover and cook on low for 7–8 hours or until all the vegetables are tender. Just before the end of cooking, add the herbs to the slow cooker pot, if using, and stir through.

3 Put the noodles in a shallow bowl, cover with boiling water and leave to soak for 4–5 minutes or cook according to the packet instructions.

4 Drain the noodles, divide between bowls and spoon the curry over the top to serve.

Tips

- **Make sure that all the pieces of potato are the same size so that they are all cooked through evenly.**

- **Do not add fish sauce if you are serving this dish to vegetarians.**

Moroccan seven

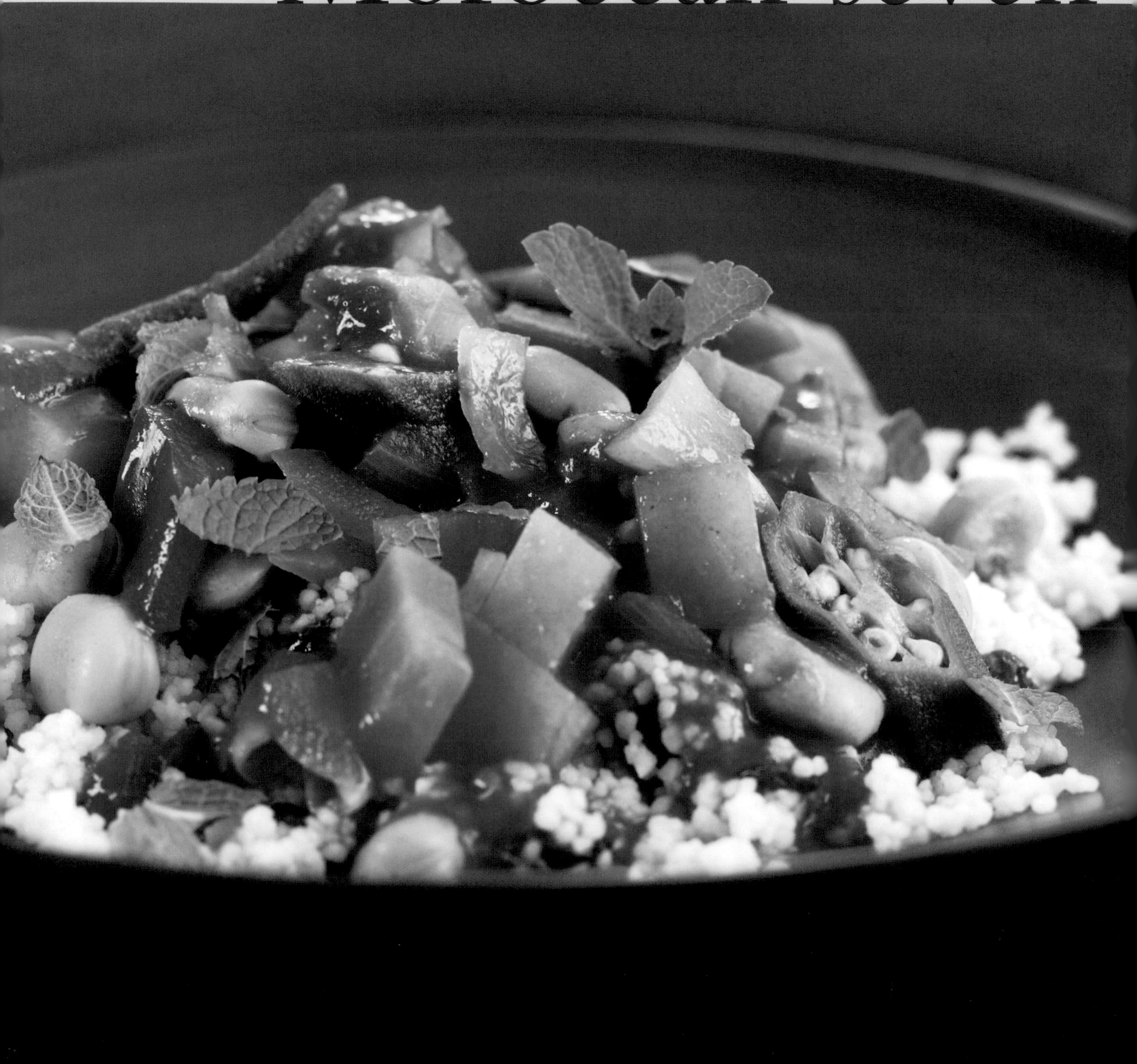

vegetable stew

The number seven is thought to be lucky in Moroccan culture, and this dish is a good way of encouraging your family to boost its intake of healthy vegetables.

Serves 4
Preparation time: 25 minutes
Cooking time: 6 hours 15 minutes–8 hours 20 minutes
Cooking temperature: low and high
Slow cooker size: standard round or oval

2 tablespoons olive oil
1 large onion, chopped
2 carrots
300 g (10 oz) swede
1 red pepper, cored, deseeded and chopped
3 garlic cloves, finely chopped
200 g (7 oz) frozen broad beans
400 g (13 oz) can chopped tomatoes
3 teaspoons harissa (chilli paste)
1 teaspoon ground turmeric
2 cm (¾ inch) fresh root ginger, peeled and
  finely chopped
250 ml (8 fl oz) vegetable stock
125 g (4 oz) okra, thickly sliced
salt and pepper
mint leaves, to garnish (optional)
couscous, to serve

1 Preheat the slow cooker if necessary – see manufacturer's instructions. Heat the oil in a large frying pan, add the onion and fry, stirring, for 5 minutes or until lightly browned.

2 Stir in the carrots, swede, red pepper, garlic, broad beans and tomatoes. Mix in the harissa, turmeric and ginger, then pour on the stock and season with salt and pepper. Bring to the boil, stirring.

3 Spoon the mixture into the slow cooker pot and press the vegetables beneath the surface of the stock. Cover and cook on low for 6–8 hours or until the root vegetables are tender.

4 Stir in the okra, cover and cook on high for 15–20 minutes or until the okra are tender but still bright green. Garnish with torn mint leaves, if using, and serve with couscous soaked in boiling water and flavoured with olive oil, lemon juice and sultanas.

Tips

• Harissa, a paste made from chillies, oil, garlic and coriander, is widely available in supermarkets.

• Cut the carrot and swede into pieces that are the same size so that they will be cooked through evenly.

Spiced date pilaf

This rice dish makes a great main course for vegetarians. Alternatively, serve it with roasted chicken or barbecued chicken kebabs.

Serves 4
Preparation time: 15 minutes
Cooking time: 2–2¼ hours
Cooking temperature: low
Slow cooker size: standard round or oval

50 g (2 oz) butter
1 onion, finely chopped
2 garlic cloves, finely chopped
1 cinnamon stick, halved
6 cardamom pods, crushed
4 whole cloves
1 bay leaf
1 teaspoon ground turmeric
250 g (8 oz) easy-cook, long-grain brown rice
750 ml (1¼ pints) hot vegetable stock
50 g (2 oz) stoned dates, chopped
50 g (2 oz) raisins
salt and pepper

1 Preheat the slow cooker if necessary – see manufacturer's instructions. Heat the butter in a frying pan, add the onion and fry gently, stirring, for 5 minutes or until softened.

2 Stir in the garlic, cinnamon, cardamom pods and seeds, cloves and bay leaf. Cook for 1 minute, then mix in the turmeric and rice and cook for 1 more minute.

3 Transfer the mixture to the slow cooker pot, pour in the hot stock, then add the dried fruits and season with salt and pepper. Stir together and cover.

4 Cook the pilaf on low for 2–2¼ hours or until the rice is tender and has absorbed nearly all the stock. Stir and spoon on to plates.

Winter vegetable ragout with lager

Serves 4

Preparation time: 30 minutes
Cooking time: 9¼–10¼ hours
Cooking temperature: low and high
Slow cooker size: standard round or oval

40 g (1½ oz) butter
1 tablespoon sunflower oil
200 g (7 oz) shallots, halved
1 leek, thinly sliced (keep white and green slices
  separate)
25 g (1 oz) plain flour
325 ml (11 fl oz) lager
300 ml (½ pint) vegetable stock
3 teaspoons wholegrain mustard
375 g (12 oz) swede
375 g (12 oz) parsnips
375 g (12 oz) carrots
1 sheet ready-rolled puff pastry, about 200 g (7 oz),
  thawed if frozen
beaten egg, to glaze
100 g (3½ oz) strong Cheddar cheese, grated
salt and pepper

1 Preheat the slow cooker if necessary – see manufacturer's instructions. Heat 15 g (½ oz) butter and oil in a large frying pan, add the shallots and white leek slices and fry until lightly browned. Scoop the onions and leeks out of the pan with a slotted spoon and transfer to a plate.

2 Melt the remaining butter and stir in the flour. Gradually mix in the lager and stock. Stir in the mustard, season with salt and pepper and bring to the boil, stirring.

3 Cut the root vegetables into 2 cm (¾ inch) dice and put them in the slow cooker pot. Add the fried shallots and leeks and pour the lager sauce over the top. Press the vegetables beneath the surface of the liquid, cover and cook on low for 9–10 hours.

4 Unroll the pastry, cut it into quarters and transfer to an oiled baking sheet. Brush with the egg and sprinkle with a little of the cheese. Bake in a preheated oven, 200°C (400°F), Gas Mark 6, for 12–15 minutes or until well risen and golden. Stir the remaining cheese and green leek slices into the slow cooker pot. Cook on high for 15 minutes.

5 Spoon the vegetables into bowls and top each with a puff pastry lid.

Mixed beans with

This garlicky, ruby-red vegetarian feast is topped with French bread toast, crumbled feta cheese and rosemary.

Serves 4

Preparation time: 20 minutes
Cooking time: 6–8 hours
Cooking temperature: low
Slow cooker size: standard round or oval

1 tablespoon olive oil
1 onion, chopped
5 small raw beetroot, about 500 g (1 lb) in total, trimmed, peeled and cut into 1 cm (½ inch) cubes
2 carrots, about 200 g (7 oz) in total, diced
2 garlic cloves, finely chopped
450 ml (¾ pint) vegetable or chicken stock
200 g (7 oz) red cabbage, shredded and woody core discarded
410 g (13¼ oz) can mixed beans, drained
1 bay leaf
2 tablespoons red wine vinegar
1 tablespoon caster sugar
salt and pepper

Topping

12 thin slices of French stick
150 g (5 oz) feta cheese, drained
1 tablespoon finely chopped rosemary leaves
2 tablespoons olive oil

1 Preheat the slow cooker if necessary – see manufacturer's instructions. Heat the oil in a large frying pan, add the onion and fry, stirring, for 5 minutes or until lightly browned. Stir in the beetroot, carrots and garlic and cook for 3 minutes. Pour in the stock and bring to the boil.

2 Transfer the beetroot mixture to the slow cooker pot. Add the red cabbage, drained beans, bay leaf and season to taste with salt and pepper. Press the vegetables beneath the surface of the liquid, cover and cook on low for 6–8 hours or until the beetroot is cooked.

3 Stir in the vinegar and sugar and replace the lid. Continue cooking until ready to serve.

4 Meanwhile, make the toasts. Put the bread slices under the grill until lightly browned on both sides. Crumble the cheese on top, sprinkle with rosemary and a little black pepper and press them down on the toast with the back of a fork. Drizzle with the oil and grill for a few more minutes or until hot. Arrange the toast on top of the beetroot mixture, lift the pot from the slow cooker and transfer it to the table.

Tip
- **Garlic and herb cream cheese or crumbled Stilton would make delicious alternative toppings for the toast.**

feta and rosemary toasts

Mixed mushroom

This hearty vegetarian main course is made with three types of mushroom simmered with Puy lentils in a tomato sauce. Serve with soft, buttery polenta and a rocket salad.

Serves 4
Preparation time: 25 minutes
Cooking time: 6–8 hours
Cooking temperature: low
Slow cooker size: standard round or oval

2 tablespoons olive oil, plus extra to serve
1 large onion, chopped
3 garlic cloves, finely chopped
400 g (13 oz) can chopped tomatoes
300 ml (½ pint) vegetable stock
150 ml (¼ pint) red wine (or extra stock)
1 tablespoon tomato purée
2 teaspoons caster sugar
salt and pepper
125 g (4 oz) Puy lentils
375 g (12 oz) cup mushrooms, halved or
  quartered depending on size
125 g (4 oz) shiitake mushrooms, halved if large
4 large field mushrooms, about 250 g (8 oz) in
  total, left whole
fried polenta, to serve

To garnish
rocket leaves
Parmesan cheese shavings

Tip
• **The mushrooms will completely fill the slow cooker when you first add them, but as they cook they will lose their bulk and simmer gently in the sauce.**

1 Preheat the slow cooker if necessary – see manufacturer's instructions. Heat the oil in a large frying pan, add the onion and fry, stirring, for 5 minutes or until lightly browned. Mix in the garlic, tomatoes, stock, wine, if using, tomato purée, sugar and season with salt and pepper. Add the Puy lentils and bring to the boil.

2 Put the mushrooms in the slow cooker pot, pour over the lentil mixture, cover and cook on low for 6–8 hours, stirring once if possible.

3 Garnish with rocket leaves tossed with Parmesan shavings and a drizzle of olive oil and serve with fried rounds of polenta.

and lentil braise

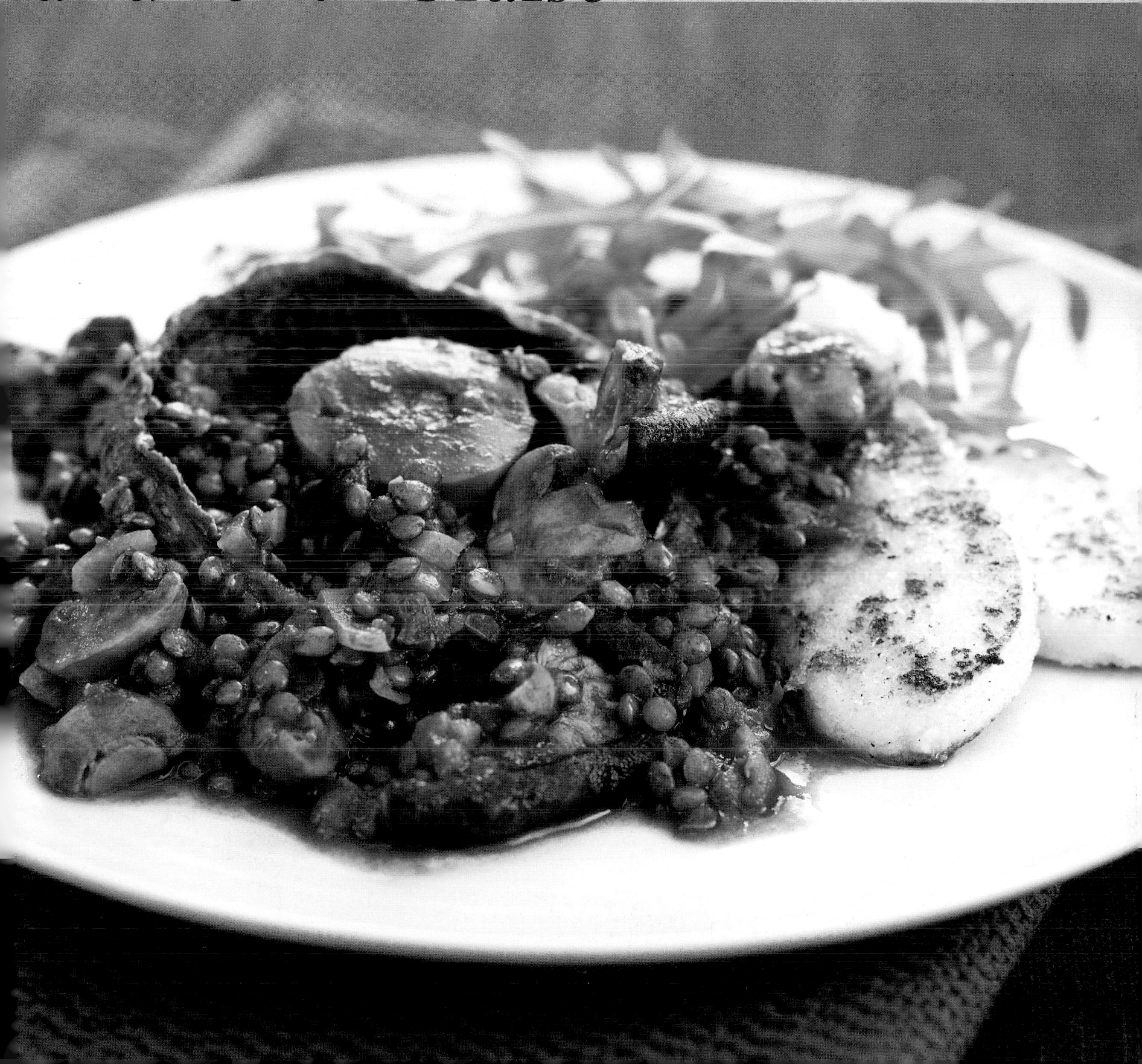

One-pot
suppers

Saffron and wild

Meaty cod loins are cooked above a delicately perfumed mix of risotto and black wild rice grains for a relaxed supper dish to share with friends.

Serves 4

Preparation time: 25 minutes
Cooking time: 1¾–2 hours
Cooking temperature: low
Slow cooker size: standard oval or round

25 g (1 oz) butter
1 tablespoon olive oil
1 onion, chopped
2 garlic cloves, finely chopped
40 g (1½ oz) wild rice
250 g (8 oz) risotto rice
2 large pinches of saffron
grated rind of 1 lemon
1.2 litres (2 pints) hot fish or vegetable stock
2 large cod loins, about 500 g (1 lb) in total
salt and pepper
basil leaves, to garnish

1 Preheat the slow cooker if necessary – see manufacturer's instructions. Heat the butter and oil in a large frying pan, add the onion and fry gently for 5 minutes or until softened but not coloured. Stir in the garlic and cook for 2 minutes.

2 Stir in the wild rice, risotto rice, saffron and lemon rind. Add the stock and bring to the boil.

3 Pour the rice mixture into the slow cooker pot, season to taste with salt and pepper and add the cod, pressing the fish just beneath the surface of the stock. Cover and cook on low for 1¾–2 hours or until the rice is cooked and has absorbed most of the stock.

4 Break each cod loin in half, spoon the rice and fish into shallow bowls, sprinkle with basil leaves and serve immediately.

Tips

- **You could add 150 ml (¼ pint) dry white wine instead of the same quantity of stock.**

- **Don't use highly seasoned stock cubes or they will overpower the delicate saffron flavour. One stock cube dissolved in 1.2 litres (2 pints) boiling water will give plenty of flavour.**

- **Don't keep risotto waiting longer than is absolutely necessary or the rice will go very sticky.**

rice risotto with cod

Lamb, port and

This classic and flavour-filled hotpot is cooked with ruby port and dried cranberries. Although a slow cooker will not brown the potatoes, you can pop the pot under the grill for a few minutes before serving.

Serves 4

Preparation time: 35 minutes
Cooking time: 7–8 hours
Cooking temperature: high
Slow cooker size: standard round or oval

1 tablespoon sunflower oil
6 lamb chump chops, about 750 g (1½ lb) in
   total, halved
1 onion, chopped
125 g (4 oz) button mushrooms, sliced
2 tablespoons plain flour
450 ml (¾ pint) lamb stock
125 ml (4 fl oz) ruby port
1 tablespoon tomato purée
1 tablespoon cranberry sauce
25 g (1 oz) dried cranberries (optional)
700 g (1 lb 7 oz) baking potatoes, thinly sliced
salt and pepper
chopped parsley, to garnish (optional)

1 Preheat the slow cooker if necessary – see manufacturer's instructions. Heat the oil in a large frying pan, add the lamb and fry over a high heat until browned on both sides. Lift out with a draining spoon and transfer to a plate.

2 Add the onion to the pan and fry, stirring, for 5 minutes or until lightly browned. Add the mushrooms and cook for 2 minutes. Stir in the flour, then gradually mix in the stock and port. Add the tomato purée, cranberry sauce and dried cranberries, if using, and season to taste with salt and pepper. Bring to the boil, stirring.

3 Put the pieces of lamb in the base of the slow cooker pot, pour over the hot sauce and arrange the sliced potatoes on top, overlapping the slices in two layers. Gently press the potatoes down into the sauce, cover and cook on high for 7–8 hours or until the lamb and potatoes are tender. Sprinkle with parsley, if liked, and spoon into bowls.

Tip

• **If you have an oven with a grill element you might like to brown the top of the potatoes before serving. Dot them with a little butter and transfer the slow cooker pot to the oven for 4–5 minutes.**

cranberry hotpot

Glazed gammon
with split pea purée

Serves 4

Preparation time: 30 minutes, plus soaking
Cooking time: 6–7 hours
Cooking temperature: high
Slow cooker size: standard oval

1.25 kg (2½ lb) boneless smoked gammon joint
200 g (7 oz) dried yellow split peas
1 large onion, roughly chopped
2 carrots, sliced
5 cloves
2 bay leaves
1.2 litres (2 pints) water

To glaze

2 teaspoons Dijon mustard
2 tablespoons maple syrup

1 Put the gammon joint in a bowl, cover with cold water and transfer to the refrigerator. Put the split peas in a second bowl, cover with cold water and leave at room temperature. Soak both overnight.

2 Preheat the slow cooker if necessary – see manufacturer's instructions. Drain the peas and put them in a saucepan with the onion, carrots, cloves, bay leaves and the measured water. Bring to the boil and boil rapidly for 10 minutes, skimming off any scum.

3 Drain the gammon joint and put it in the slow cooker pot. Pour the water and pea mixture over the top, cover and cook on high for 6–7 hours or until the peas are soft and the gammon is tender.

4 Lift the gammon out of the pot, put it in a grill pan and cut away the rind. Spread the mustard over the fat, then drizzle with the maple syrup. Cook under the grill until the fat is golden.

5 Meanwhile, drain off most of the stock from the peas but reserve the liquid. Mash the peas and spoon them on to plates. Slice the gammon and arrange on top, and serve with a little of the reserved ham stock if liked.

Tip
- **You can use honey to glaze the gammon if you do not have any maple syrup.**

Bigos

Popular in eastern Europe, this pork casserole is flavoured with sauerkraut, paprika and caraway seeds and served with chunky pieces of pork, smoked pork sausage and pickled cucumbers.

Serves 4

Preparation time: 30 minutes
Cooking time: 8–10 hours
Cooking temperature: low
Slow cooker size: standard round or oval

625 g (1¼ lb) lean pork belly
1 tablespoon sunflower oil
1 large onion, roughly chopped
1 teaspoon paprika
1 teaspoon caraway seeds
400 g (13 oz) can chopped tomatoes
450 ml (¾ pint) chicken stock
2 dessert apples, cored and diced (skins left on)
225 g (7½ oz) smoked pork sausage, thickly sliced
150 g (5 oz) pickled dill cucumbers, drained and
   thickly sliced
375 g (12 oz) sauerkraut, drained
salt and pepper
bread, to serve

1 Preheat the slow cooker if necessary – see manufacturer's instructions. Remove the rind from the pork and dice the meat. Heat the oil in a large frying pan, add the onion and pork and fry until lightly browned.

2 Stir in the paprika and caraway seeds, then mix in the tomatoes and stock. Season to taste with salt and pepper and bring to the boil, stirring.

3 Put the apples, smoked pork sausage and dill cucumbers into the slow cooker pot. Pour over the pork and onion mixture, then spoon the sauerkraut on top. Cover and cook on low for 8–10 hours.

4 Stir and spoon into shallow bowls. Serve with bread and spoons to scoop up the sauce.

Tip
- **The pork sausage, which is shaped like a horseshoe, is sometimes known as smoked pork boiling ring. If you cannot get this use a spiced sausage such as kabanos.**

Pot-roast guinea

Serves 4

Preparation time: 30 minutes
Cooking time: 5¼–6¼ hours
Cooking temperature: high
Slow cooker size: standard oval

1 tablespoon olive oil
25 g (1 oz) butter
1 guinea fowl, about 1 kg (2 lb)
1 large onion, cut into thin wedges
2 leeks, thickly sliced (keep white and green
   slices separate)
2 garlic cloves, finely chopped
200 ml (7 fl oz) dry white wine
2 teaspoons Dijon mustard
500 g (1 lb) baby new potatoes, thickly sliced
200 g (7 oz) carrots, sliced
900 ml (1½ pints) hot chicken stock
150 g (5 oz) hulled broad beans, thawed if frozen
salt and pepper

Salsa verde

25 g (1 oz) flat leaf parsley, chopped
2 garlic cloves, finely chopped
3 tablespoons olive oil
2 teaspoons white wine vinegar

1 Preheat the slow cooker if necessary – see manufacturer's instructions. Heat the oil and butter in a frying pan, add the guinea fowl breast side downwards and fry until golden. Turn and brown the underside. Lift out and put on to a plate.

2 Add the onion and white sliced leeks and fry for 5 minutes. Add the garlic and cook for 2 minutes, then stir in the wine and mustard, season with salt and pepper, and bring to the boil.

3 Put the guinea fowl into the slow cooker pot, breast side uppermost. Tuck the potatoes and carrots down the sides of the bird. Pour over the hot onion, leek and wine mixture, then add the hot stock. Make sure that the potatoes and carrots are below the stock level. Cover and cook on high for 5–6 hours or until the guinea fowl and vegetables are tender. Check the guinea fowl by inserting a knife through the thickest part of the leg into the breast meat. The juices will run clear when the bird is ready.

4 Lift the guinea fowl out of the pot, put it on a plate and wrap in foil to keep hot. Add the green sliced leeks and broad beans to the pot and cook on high for 15 minutes. Meanwhile, mix together the salsa verde ingredients in a small bowl.

5 Spoon the vegetables and some of the stock into serving bowls. Carve the guinea fowl and add it to the bowls with spoonfuls of salsa verde.

fowl with salsa verde

Turkey carbonnade
with polenta squares

Serves 4

Preparation time: 30 minutes
Cooking time: 8–10 hours
Cooking temperature: low
Slow cooker size: standard round or oval

1 tablespoon olive oil
500 g (1 lb) minced turkey
1 large onion, roughly chopped
2 garlic cloves, finely chopped
1 large carrot, cut into small dice
2 tablespoons plain flour
400 g (13 oz) can chopped tomatoes
300 ml (½ pint) chicken stock
50 g (2 oz) sun-dried tomatoes, drained and
    thickly sliced
2–3 sprigs of rosemary
salt and pepper
rocket salad, to serve

Polenta

850 ml (30 fl oz) boiling water
150 g (5 oz) quick-cook polenta
50 g (2 oz) butter
3 tablespoons grated Parmesan cheese, plus extra
    to garnish
2 tablespoons olive oil

1 Preheat the slow cooker if necessary – see manufacturer's instructions. Heat the oil in a large frying pan, add the meat and onion and fry over a high heat, stirring, for 5 minutes or until browned. Stir in the garlic and carrot and cook for 2 minutes.

2 Mix in the flour, then add the canned tomatoes, stock, sun-dried tomatoes and rosemary. Season with salt and pepper and bring to the boil, stirring to break up any large clumps of mince. Spoon the mixture into the slow cooker pot, press the mince below the surface of the liquid, cover and cook on low for 8–10 hours.

3 Prepare the polenta. Bring the measured water to the boil in a saucepan, add the polenta, bring back to the boil and cook, stirring, for 1–2 minutes or until thick. Remove from the heat, add the butter, Parmesan and plenty of salt and pepper and stir until the butter has melted. Pour into an oiled 20 cm (8 inch) shallow cake tin or small roasting tin, spread into an even layer and leave to cool and set.

4 Cut the polenta into 12 pieces, heat the oil in a large frying pan and fry the polenta until it is hot and golden. Arrange pieces overlapping around the edge of the mince, sprinkle with a little extra Parmesan and serve with a rocket salad.

Summer garden pie

This comforting midweek supper dish is made with diced chicken thighs simmered with diced bacon, wholegrain mustard and finished with a colourful mix of fresh vegetables topped with tasty mashed potatoes.

Serves 6

Preparation time: 30 minutes
Cooking time: 6 hours 20 minutes–8 hours 20 minutes
Cooking temperature: low and high
Slow cooker size: standard round or oval

8 chicken thighs, about 1 kg (2 lb) in total
1 tablespoon sunflower oil
1 onion, chopped
2 rashers of smoked back bacon, diced
2 tablespoons plain flour
450 ml (¾ pint) chicken stock
2 teaspoons wholegrain mustard
2 carrots, diced
2 courgettes, diced
150 g (5 oz) runner beans, topped and tailed and
   cut into thin strips
100 g (3½ oz) fresh or frozen peas
salt and pepper

Mustard mash

1 kg (2 lb) potatoes
40 g (1½ oz) butter
2–4 tablespoons milk
2 teaspoons wholegrain mustard
40 g (1½ oz) strong Cheddar cheese, grated

1 Preheat the slow cooker if necessary – see manufacturer's instructions. Cut the skin away from the chicken thighs, remove the bones and cut the meat into chunks.

2 Heat the oil in a large frying pan, add the chicken, a few pieces at a time, until all the meat is in the pan, then add the onion and bacon. Fry, stirring, for 5 minutes or until lightly browned.

3 Mix in the flour, then add the stock, mustard and carrots. Season to taste with salt and pepper; bring to the boil and transfer to the slow cooker pot. Cover and cook on low for 6–8 hours.

4 Add the green vegetables to the slow cooker, replace the lid and cook on high for 20 minutes or until tender.

5 Meanwhile, cook the potatoes in a saucepan of boiling water until tender. Drain and mash with the butter and milk. Stir in the mustard and salt and pepper to taste. Spoon the potato over the top of the slow cooker pot and sprinkle with the cheese. Grill, if liked, to brown the top of the pie.

Caribbean chicken

with rice and peas

There are as many versions of rice and peas as there are types of peas and beans. Here red kidney beans, white long-grain rice and frozen green peas are added to chicken thighs spread with spicy jerk marinade and simmered in coconut milk.

Serves 4
Preparation time: 20 minutes
Cooking time: 7–9 hours
Cooking temperature: low and high
Slow cooker size: standard round or oval

8 chicken thighs, about 1 kg (2 lb) in total
3 tablespoons jerk marinade (see tip below)
2 tablespoons sunflower oil
2 large onions, chopped
2 garlic cloves, finely chopped
400 ml (14 fl oz) can reduced-fat coconut milk
300 ml (½ pint) chicken stock
410 g (13½ oz) can red kidney beans, drained
200 g (7 oz) easy-cook, white long-grain rice
125 g (4 oz) frozen peas
salt and pepper
To garnish
lime wedges
coriander sprigs

1 Preheat the slow cooker if necessary – see manufacturer's instructions. Remove the skin from the chicken thighs, slash each thigh two or three times and rub with the jerk marinade.

2 Heat 1 tablespoon oil in a large frying pan, add the chicken and fry over a high heat until browned on both sides. Lift out and transfer to a plate. Add the remaining oil, the onions and garlic, reduce the heat and fry for 5 minutes or until softened and lightly browned. Pour in the coconut milk and stock, season with salt and pepper and bring the mixture to the boil.

3 Transfer half the mixture to the slow cooker pot, add half the chicken pieces, all the beans and then the remaining chicken, onions and coconut mixture. Cover and cook on low for 6–8 hours or until the chicken is tender.

4 Stir in the rice, replace the lid and cook on high for 45 minutes. Add the frozen peas (no need to defrost) and cook for 15 minutes more. Spoon on to plates and garnish with lime wedges and coriander sprigs.

Tip
• **Jerk marinade is a spicy dark brown paste, and you will find jars of it in most large supermarkets.**

Peppered venison

Serves 4–5

Preparation time: 35 minutes
Cooking time: 8¾–11 hours
Cooking temperature: low and high
Slow cooker size: standard round or oval

25 g (1 oz) butter
1 tablespoon olive oil
750 g (1½ lb) venison shoulder, diced
1 large red onion, sliced
125 g (4 oz) cup mushrooms, sliced
2 garlic cloves, finely chopped (optional)
2 tablespoons plain flour
200 ml (7 fl oz) red wine
250 ml (8 fl oz) lamb or chicken stock
2 teaspoons tomato purée
2 tablespoons redcurrant jelly
1 teaspoon peppercorns, roughly crushed
salt and pepper
green beans, to serve

Scones

250 g (8 oz) self-raising flour
40 g (1½ oz) butter, diced
125 g (4 oz) Gorgonzola cheese, rind removed
  and diced
3 tablespoons chopped parsley or chives
1 egg, beaten
4–5 tablespoons milk

1 Preheat the slow cooker if necessary – see manufacturer's instructions. Heat the butter and oil in a large frying pan, add the diced venison, a few pieces at time, until all the meat has been added, then fry until evenly browned. Transfer to a plate.

2 Add the onion and fry for 5 minutes. Stir in the mushrooms, garlic, if using, and flour and cook for 1 minute. Stir in the wine, stock, tomato purée, redcurrant jelly, peppercorns and salt and bring to the boil.

3 Spoon the venison into the pot, add the hot wine mixture and press the venison below the surface. Cover and cook on low for 8–10 hours.

4 Make the scones. Place the flour in a bowl, add the butter and rub in with the fingertips until the mixture resembles fine breadcrumbs. Stir in a little salt and pepper, the cheese and herbs. Reserve 1 tablespoon of egg for glazing and add the rest. Gradually mix in enough milk to make a soft dough.

5 Lightly knead, then pat the dough into a thick oval or a round that is a little smaller than the top of your slow cooker. Cut it into 8 wedges and arrange, spaced slightly apart, on top of the venison. Cover and cook on high for ¾–1 hour.

6 Brush the scones with the reserved egg and brown under the grill. Serve with green beans.

with nutty crumble

Feta tiganito

Garlicky fried layers of sliced aubergine, peppers and a rich tomato sauce are topped with melting feta cheese. Serve with warm pitta breads and salad.

Serves 4–5

Preparation time: 30 minutes
Cooking time: 5–6 hours
Cooking temperature: high
Slow cooker size: standard round or oval

2 large aubergines, thickly sliced
4–5 tablespoons olive oil
2 onions, roughly chopped
3 garlic cloves, finely chopped
2 × 400 g (13 oz) cans chopped tomatoes
2 teaspoons caster sugar
large pinch of grated nutmeg
small bunch of oregano or basil
2 peppers (red and orange), cored, deseeded
  and diced
150 g (5 oz) feta cheese, drained and crumbled
40 g (1½ oz) pitted black olives
salt and pepper

To serve

toasted pitta bread
green salad

1 Preheat the slow cooker if necessary – see manufacturer's instructions. Lay the aubergine slices on a tray, sprinkle with salt and set aside for 15–20 minutes or until the juices begin to run.

2 Heat 1 tablespoon oil of in a saucepan, add the onions and fry until just beginning to brown. Add the garlic, fry for 1 minute, then mix in the tomatoes, sugar and nutmeg. Season to taste with salt and pepper. Tear half the herbs into small pieces and add them to the sauce.

3 Rinse the aubergine slices under cold water to remove the salt, drain them well and dry with kitchen paper. Heat a little of the remaining oil in a large frying pan and fry the aubergine slices in batches, adding more oil as needed, until browned on both sides. Transfer to a plate.

4 Layer the aubergines, peppers, feta and hot sauce alternately in the slow cooker pot, finishing with a thick layer of sauce and feta. Sprinkle the olives on top, cover and cook on high for 5–6 hours. Spoon into shallow bowls, garnish with the remaining herb leaves and serve with toasted pitta bread and a green salad.

Mixed vegetable bourride

Saffron adds a delicate flavour to this Mediterranean mix of peppers, plum tomatoes, courgettes and cannellini beans. Serve in shallow soup bowls topped with toasted French bread and rouille and eat with forks and spoons to scoop up the garlicky sauce.

Serves 4

Preparation time: 30 minutes
Cooking time: 6½–8¾ hours
Cooking temperature: low and high
Slow cooker size: standard round or oval

1 tablespoon olive oil
1 large red onion, roughly chopped
3 peppers (red, yellow and orange), cored, deseeded and diced
2–3 garlic cloves, finely chopped
500 g (1 lb) plum tomatoes, peeled if liked, diced
410 g (13½ oz) can cannellini beans, drained
150 ml (¼ pint) dry white wine
150 ml (¼ pint) vegetable stock
2 large pinches of saffron threads
2 teaspoons caster sugar
400 g (13 oz) courgettes, cubed
salt and pepper

To serve

1 red chilli, halved, deseeded and finely chopped
2 garlic cloves, finely chopped .
4 tablespoons mayonnaise
1 small baguette or ½ French stick, sliced

1 Preheat the slow cooker if necessary – see manufacturer's instructions. Heat the oil in a large frying pan, add the onion and fry, stirring, for 5 minutes or until lightly browned. Add the peppers and garlic and fry for 2 minutes.

2 Mix in the tomatoes, beans, wine, stock, saffron and sugar. Season to taste with salt and pepper, then bring to the boil and spoon into the slow cooker pot. Press the vegetables beneath the liquid, cover and cook on low for 6–8 hours or until the vegetables are tender.

3 Stir the courgettes into the slow cooker pot and cook on high for 30–45 minutes or until they are just tender but still bright green.

4 Meanwhile, mix the chilli and garlic into the mayonnaise. Toast the bread just before serving. Ladle the bourride into shallow soup bowls, top with the toast and spoon a little rouille on to each slice.

Tip

• **Rouille is a reddish, chilli-based sauce from the south of France, which is traditionally served with fish stews but is also delicious with vegetables.**

Rosemary pudding with

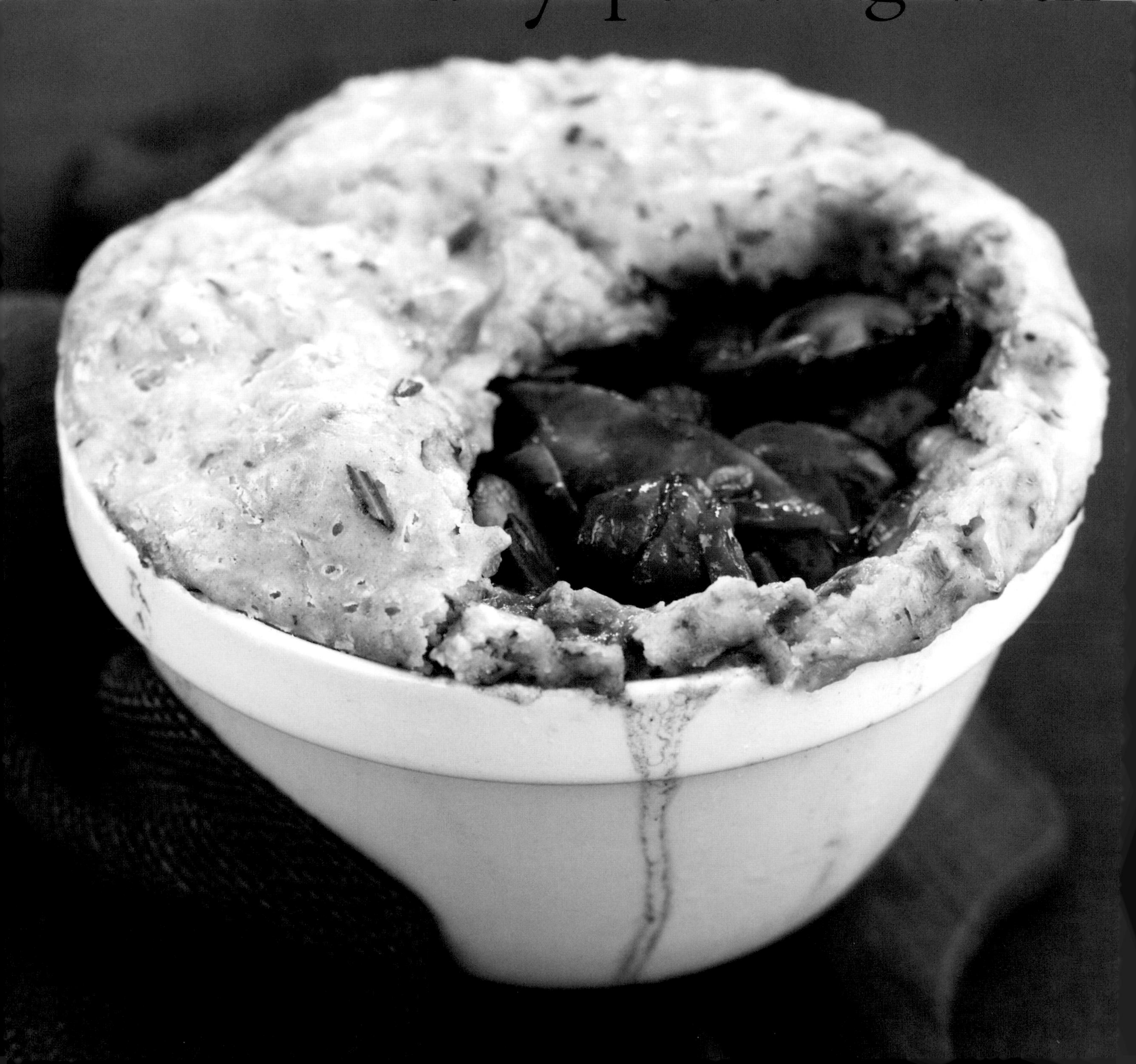

mushrooms and chestnuts

Serves 4

Preparation time: 45 minutes
Cooking time: 5–6 hours
Cooking temperature: high
Slow cooker size: standard oval

Sauce

15 g (½ oz) butter
1 tablespoon sunflower oil
1 onion, thinly sliced
1 tablespoon plain flour
300 ml (½ pint) vegetable stock
5 tablespoons ruby port
1 teaspoon Dijon mustard
1 teaspoon tomato purée
salt and pepper

Pastry

300 g (10 oz) self-raising flour
½ teaspoon salt
150 g (5 oz) shredded vegetable suet
2 tablespoons finely chopped rosemary leaves
about 200 ml (7 fl oz) cold water

Filling

1 large flat mushroom, sliced
125 g (4 oz) chestnut cup mushrooms, sliced
200 g (7 oz) vacuum pack whole peeled chestnuts

1 Preheat the slow cooker if necessary – see manufacturer's instructions. Make the sauce. Heat the butter and oil in a large frying pan, add the onion and fry for 5 minutes. Stir in the flour, then mix in the stock, port, mustard and tomato purée. Add salt and pepper, bring to the boil, stirring, then take off the heat.

2 Make the pastry. Mix together the flour, salt, suet and rosemary. Gradually add enough cold water to mix to a soft but not sticky dough. Knead lightly, then roll out to a circle 33 cm (13 inches) across.

3 Cut a one-quarter segment from the circle of pastry and reserve. Lift the remaining pastry into an oiled 1.25 litre (2¼ pint) pudding basin and bring the cut edges together, overlapping them slightly so that the basin is completely lined with pastry, then press them together to seal. Layer the sauce, mushrooms and chestnuts into the basin, finishing with the sauce.

4 Pat the reserved pastry into a circle the same size as the top of the basin. Dampen the edges of the pastry in the basin with a little water and press the lid in place. Cover with buttered foil and dome the foil slightly. Tie in place with string, then lower into the slow cooker pot with a string handle (see page 13).

5 Pour boiling water into the slow cooker pot so that it comes halfway up the sides of the basin. Cover and cook on high for 5–6 hours.

Just desserts

Serves 4–5

Preparation time: 30 minutes
Cooking time: 3–3½ hours
Cooking temperature: high
Slow cooker size: standard oval

50 g (2 oz) butter, diced, plus extra for greasing
150 g (5 oz) self-raising flour
100 g (3½ oz) dark muscovado sugar
2 eggs
2 tablespoons milk
1 dessert apple, cored and finely chopped
vanilla ice cream, crème fraîche or pouring cream,
   to serve

Sauce

125 g (4 oz) dark muscovado sugar
25 g (1 oz) butter, diced
300 ml (½ pint) boiling water

1 Preheat the slow cooker if necessary – see manufacturer's instructions. Butter the inside of a soufflé dish that is 14 cm (5½ inches) across and 9 cm (3½ inches) high. Put the flour in a bowl, add the butter and rub in with the fingertips until the mixture resembles fine breadcrumbs. Stir in the sugar, then mix in the eggs and milk until smooth. Stir in the apple.

2 Spoon the mixture into the soufflé dish and spread it level. Sprinkle the sugar for the sauce over the top and dot with the 25 g (1 oz) butter. Pour the measured boiling water over the top, then loosely cover with foil.

3 Carefully lower the dish into the slow cooker pot using a string handle or foil straps (see page 13). Pour boiling water into the pot so that it comes halfway up the sides of the soufflé dish. Cover and cook on high for 3–3½ hours or until the sponge is well risen and the sauce is bubbling around the edges.

4 Lift the dish out of the slow cooker. Remove the foil and loosen the sides of the sponge. Cover with a dish that is large enough to catch the sauce, invert and remove the soufflé dish. Serve with spoonfuls of vanilla ice cream, crème fraîche or pouring cream.

Tip
• **Check that the soufflé dish will fit in your slow cooker pot before you begin.**

apple pudding

Rum and raisin spotted dick

Serves 8

Preparation time: 20 minutes, plus soaking
Cooking time: 3–4 hours
Cooking temperature: high
Slow cooker size: standard oval

200 g (7 oz) raisins
5 tablespoons dark rum
butter, for greasing
200 g (7 oz) self-raising flour
50 g (2 oz) fresh white breadcrumbs
100 g (3½ oz) light vegetable suet
100 g (3½ oz) caster sugar
finely grated rind and juice of 1 orange
1 egg
150 ml (¼ pint) milk

To serve

golden syrup
custard

1 Put the raisins in a bowl, add the rum and leave to soak overnight.

2 Preheat the slow cooker if necessary – see manufacturer's instructions. Butter a 1.25 litre (2¼ pint) pudding basin and line the base with a circle of greaseproof paper. Put the flour, breadcrumbs, suet, sugar and orange rind in a mixing bowl. Add the raisins and any remaining rum, the orange juice and egg, then gradually mix in enough milk to make a soft, dropping consistency.

3 Spoon the mixture into the basin, level the surface and cover with a piece of pleated greaseproof paper and foil. Tie the foil in place with string and lower the basin into the base of the slow cooker pot using string handles (see page 13). Pour boiling water into the slow cooker pot so that it comes halfway up the side of the basin, cover and cook on high for 3–4 hours or until the pudding is well risen and cooked through.

4 Loosen the sides of the pudding, turn it out on to a plate and peel away the lining paper. Serve with golden syrup and custard.

Tips

- **If you're short of time, warm the rum and raisins in a saucepan or in the microwave and leave to soak for 2 hours.**

- **When there's not enough bread to make into breadcrumbs, use 275 g (9 oz) self-raising flour, although the texture of the pudding will be a little heavier.**

110

Butterscotch bananas

This children's favourite is incredibly quick and easy to make, and it's likely that you will already have all the ingredients in your storecupboard.

Serves 4

Preparation time: 15 minutes
Cooking time: 1–1½ hours
Cooking temperature: low
Slow cooker size: standard round or oval

4 bananas
juice of 1 lemon
50 g (2 oz) butter
75 g (3 oz) soft light brown muscovado sugar
2 tablespoons golden syrup
vanilla ice cream, to serve

1 Preheat the slow cooker if necessary – see manufacturer's instructions. Thickly slice the bananas, put them in a bowl and toss with the lemon juice.

2 Put the butter, sugar and syrup in a small saucepan and heat until the butter has melted and the sugar has dissolved.

3 Transfer the bananas to the slow cooker pot, pour the hot butter mixture over them, cover and cook on low for 1–1½ hours.

4 Spoon the bananas into glass bowls and serve with scoops of vanilla ice cream.

Black cherry and

These irresistible little puddings are made easily with a quick-mix sponge and a can of cherries from your storecupboard.

Serves 4

Preparation time: 25 minutes
Cooking time: 1½–2 hours
Cooking temperature: high
Slow cooker size: standard oval

50 g (2 oz) butter, plus extra for greasing
50 g (2 oz) caster sugar
50 g (2 oz) self-raising flour
1 egg
1 tablespoon cocoa powder
¼ teaspoon baking powder
¼ teaspoon ground cinnamon
425 g (14 oz) can pitted black cherries, drained

Chocolate sauce
100 g (3½ oz) white chocolate, broken into pieces
150 ml (¼ pint) double cream

1 Preheat the slow cooker if necessary – see manufacturer's instructions. Butter the inside of 4 metal pudding moulds, each with a capacity of 200 ml (7 fl oz), and line the base of each with a circle of greaseproof paper.

2 Put the remaining butter, sugar, flour, egg, cocoa, baking powder and cinnamon in a bowl and beat them together with a wooden spoon until smooth.

3 Arrange 7 cherries in the base of each pudding mould. Roughly chop the remainder and stir them into the pudding mix. Divide the mixture among the pudding moulds and level the tops. Loosely cover the tops of the moulds with foil and put them in the slow cooker pot. Pour boiling water into the pot so that it comes halfway up the sides of the moulds, cover and cook on high for 1½–2 hours or until the puddings are well risen and the tops spring back when pressed with a fingertip. Lift the puddings out of the slow cooker pot.

4 Make the sauce. Put the chocolate and cream in a small saucepan and heat gently, stirring occasionally, until melted. Loosen the edges of the puddings, turn them out into shallow bowls, peel away the lining paper and pour the sauce around them before serving.

Tip
• **If you don't have metal moulds, you could use small teacups or coffee cups to cook the puddings but make sure that they fit into the slow cooker pot before you begin.**

chocolate puddings

Orange risotto with

This Italian dairy-free version of rice pudding is flavoured with an orange syrup and topped with flaked almonds, caramelized with a little icing sugar.

Serves 6

Preparation time: 25 minutes
Cooking time: 2½–3 hours
Cooking temperature: low
Slow cooker size: standard round or oval

5 oranges
75 g (3 oz) caster sugar
1–2 bay leaves, depending on size
1 litre (1¾ pints) water
200 g (7 oz) risotto rice
pouring cream, to serve (optional)
Caramelized almonds
15 g (½ oz) butter
40 g (1½ oz) flaked almonds
2 tablespoons icing sugar

1 Preheat the slow cooker if necessary – see manufacturer's instructions. Grate the rind from 1 orange and squeeze the juice from this and another orange. Cut the peel and pith away from the 3 remaining oranges and cut the flesh into segments. Put the segments in a small bowl, cover and set aside until ready to serve.

2 Put the orange rind and juice in a saucepan with the sugar, bay leaves and water. Bring slowly to the boil, stirring, until the sugar has completely dissolved. Boil for 1 minute.

3 Put the rice in the slow cooker pot, pour over the hot syrup and mix together. Cover and cook on low for 2½–3 hours or until the rice is tender and has absorbed most of the syrup.

4 Meanwhile, make the caramelized almonds. Melt the butter in a frying pan, add the almonds and fry, stirring, for 2–3 minutes or until golden. Mix in the sugar and cook for 1 minute.

5 Spoon the risotto into small bowls and top with the orange segments and warm nuts. Serve with a drizzle of pouring cream, if liked.

caramelized almonds

Nectarine compote

with orange mascarpone

Full of summer flavours, these lightly poached fruits are served with soft creamy mascarpone cheese flecked with crumbled almondy amaretti biscuits. Although this compote is served warm, it tastes just as good chilled.

Serves 4

Preparation time: 20 minutes
Cooking time: 1–1¼ hours
Cooking temperature: high
Slow cooker size: standard round or oval

4 nectarines
250 g (8 oz) strawberries
50 g (2 oz) caster sugar, plus 2 tablespoons
finely grated rind and juice of 2 oranges
125 ml (4 fl oz) cold water
150 g (5 oz) mascarpone cheese
40 g (1½ oz) amaretti biscuits

1 Preheat the slow cooker if necessary – see manufacturer's instructions. Halve the nectarines, remove the stones and cut the flesh into chunks. Quarter or halve the strawberries depending on their size.

2 Put the fruit in the slow cooker pot with 50 g (2 oz) sugar, the rind of 1 orange, the juice of 1½ oranges and the measured water. Cover and cook on high for 1–1¼ hours or until the fruit is tender.

3 Just before the compote is ready, mix the mascarpone cheese with the remaining sugar, orange rind and juice. Reserve some of the amaretti biscuits for decoration. Crumble the rest with your fingertips into the bowl with the mascarpone and stir until mixed. Spoon the fruit into tumblers, top with spoonfuls of the mascarpone mixture and decorate with a sprinkling of amaretti biscuits.

Tip
• Use ratafia or macaroon biscuits instead of the amaretti biscuits if you prefer.

Lemon sponge pudding

Serves 6

Preparation time: 30 minutes
Cooking time: 3–3½ hours
Cooking temperature: high
Slow cooker size: standard oval

125 g (4 oz) butter, plus extra for greasing
4 tablespoons golden syrup
100 g (3½ oz) caster sugar
grated rind of 2 lemons
2 eggs, beaten
200 g (7 oz) self-raising flour
2 tablespoons milk
2 tablespoons lemon juice
3 passion fruit

1 Preheat the slow cooker if necessary – see manufacturer's instructions. Butter the inside of a 1.25 litre (2¼ pint) pudding basin and line the base with a circle of greaseproof paper. Spoon the syrup into the basin.

2 Cream together the butter, sugar and lemon rind in a bowl until pale and creamy. Gradually mix in alternate spoonfuls of beaten egg and flour until both have been added and the mixture is smooth. Stir in the milk and then the lemon juice to make a soft, dropping consistency.

3 Spoon the mixture over the syrup in the basin. Level the surface and cover with a piece of pleated greaseproof paper and foil. Tie with string.

4 Lower the basin into the slow cooker pot (see page 13). Pour boiling water into the pot so that it comes halfway up the sides of the basin. Cover and cook on high for 3–3½ hours or until the top springs back when pressed with a fingertip.

5 Carefully lift the basin out of the slow cooker. Remove the foil and greaseproof paper and loosen the sides of the sponge. Cover with a large plate, invert the basin on to it and remove the basin and lining paper. Halve the passion fruit and scoop the seeds over the pudding.

Tip
- **For an alternative sauce, warm 4 tablespoons cranberry sauce or good strawberry jam with the juice of half an orange.**

Double chocolate
and sweet potato cake

Serves 6

Preparation time: 40 minutes
Cooking time: 3½–4 hours
Cooking temperature: high
Slow cooker size: standard oval

250 g (8 oz) sweet potato, peeled and cut into
  chunks
2 tablespoons milk
125 g (4 oz) butter, plus extra for greasing
125 g (4 oz) soft light muscovado sugar
150 g (5 oz) self-raising flour
2 tablespoons cocoa powder, plus extra to decorate
  (optional)
½ teaspoon bicarbonate of soda
2 eggs, beaten
25 g (1 oz) crystallized ginger, chopped
100 g (3½ oz) dark chocolate, diced
25 g (1 oz) pistachio nuts or hazelnuts, roughly
  chopped
cream, to serve

1 Cook the sweet potato in a saucepan of boiling water for 15 minutes or until tender. Drain and mash with the milk, then leave to cool.

2 Preheat the slow cooker if necessary – see manufacturer's instructions. Butter the inside of a soufflé dish that is 14 cm (5½ inches) across and 9 cm (3½ inches) high, line the base with greaseproof paper. Cream the butter and sugar together in a bowl until light and fluffy. Mix the flour, cocoa and bicarbonate of soda together. Gradually mix in alternate spoonfuls of egg and flour until both have been added and the mixture is smooth. Stir in the potato, ginger and chocolate.

3 Spoon the mixture into the buttered dish, level the surface and sprinkle over the nuts. Cover the top loosely with buttered foil and lower into the slow cooker pot (see page 13). Pour boiling water into the pot so that it comes halfway up the sides of the dish. Cover and cook on high for 3½–4 hours or until the cake springs back when pressed with a fingertip.

4 Loosen the cake, turn it out on to a plate and peel off the lining paper. Serve warm or cold with cream.

Marbled chocolate
and vanilla cheesecake

Serves 6

Preparation time: 40 minutes, plus chilling
Cooking time: 3–4 hours
Cooking temperature: high
Slow cooker size: standard oval

Base

50 g (2 oz) butter at room temperature, plus extra
　for greasing
50 g (2 oz) caster sugar
50 g (2 oz) self-raising flour
1 egg

Filling

100 g (3½ oz) dark chocolate, broken into pieces
250 g (8 oz) mascarpone cheese
50 g (2 oz) caster sugar
4 tablespoons full-fat crème fraîche
2 whole eggs and 2 extra yolks
1 teaspoon vanilla extract

1 Preheat the slow cooker if necessary – see manufacturer's instructions. Butter a soufflé dish that is 14 cm (5½ inches) across and 9 cm (3½ inches) high. Line the base with greaseproof paper.

2 Make the base. Put all the ingredients in a bowl and beat together until smooth. Spoon into the dish and level the surface. Cover the top loosely with foil and lower the dish into the slow cooker pot (see page 13). Pour boiling water into the pot so that it comes halfway up the sides of the dish, cover and cook on high for 1–1½ hours. Meanwhile, melt the chocolate in a heatproof bowl set over a small saucepan of simmering water. Mix the mascarpone and sugar in a bowl. Stir in the crème fraîche then gradually beat in the whole eggs, and yolks.

3 Lift the dish out of the slow cooker. Gradually stir 8 tablespoons of the cheesecake mixture into the chocolate. Stir the vanilla extract into the remaining mixture, then pour it into the sponge-lined dish. Drizzle spoonfuls of the chocolate mixture over the top, then run a knife through the mixtures to create a marbled effect. Re-cover the dish and return it to the slow cooker. Cook on high for 2–2½ hours. Lift out and cool, then refrigerate for 3–4 hours.

4 Loosen the edges of the cheesecake, turn it out, peel away the paper then turn the right way up.

Tip
- **The cheesecake will sink slightly as it cools. Don't worry – this is perfectly normal.**

Lemon custard creams

Serve this rich baked custard, made with double cream and tangy lemon rind and juice, with fresh blueberries, mixed summer fruits or cherries.

Serves 6

Preparation time: 15 minutes, plus chilling
Cooking time: 2–2½ hours
Cooking temperature: low
Slow cooker size: standard oval

2 whole eggs and 3 extra yolks
100 g (3½ oz) caster sugar
grated rind of 2 lemons
juice of 1 lemon
300 ml (½ pint) double cream
150 g (5 oz) fresh blueberries, to serve

1 Preheat the slow cooker if necessary – see manufacturer's instructions. Put the eggs and yolks, sugar and lemon rind in a bowl and whisk together until just mixed.

2 Pour the cream into a small saucepan, bring just to the boil, then gradually whisk it into the egg mixture. Strain the lemon juice and gradually whisk it into the cream mixture.

3 Pour the mixture into 6 small coffee cups and put them in the slow cooker pot. Pour boiling water into the pot so that it comes halfway up the sides of the cups. Loosely cover the tops of the cups with a piece of foil, cover and cook on low for 2–2½ hours or until the custards are just set.

4 Lift the cups from the slow cooker, leave to cool, then transfer to the refrigerator and chill well.

5 To serve, set the cups on their saucers and decorate the tops of the custard with blueberries.

Tips

- **Check that the cups will fit side by side in the pot before you begin. If you don't have any small cups, use dariole or madeleine tins or small 150 ml (¼ pint) metal moulds instead.**

- **To make these desserts into crème brûlée, sprinkle the top of each chilled dessert with 1 rounded teaspoon of caster sugar. Caramelize the sugar with a kitchen blowtorch and serve within 20 minutes.**

Sticky glazed banana

Serves 6

Preparation time: 30 minutes
Cooking time: 4–5 hours
Cooking temperature: high
Slow cooker size: standard oval

Pudding base

3 tablespoons golden syrup
3 tablespoons light muscovado sugar
1 tablespoon ginger or orange marmalade
2 bananas
juice ½ lemon

Gingerbread

100 g (3½ oz) butter, plus extra for greasing
100 g (3½ oz) light muscovado sugar
75 g (3 oz) golden syrup
2 tablespoons ginger or orange marmalade
2 eggs
4 tablespoons milk
175 g (6 oz) self-raising wholemeal flour
1 teaspoon bicarbonate of soda
2 teaspoons ground ginger
custard or vanilla ice cream, to serve

1 Preheat the slow cooker if necessary – see manufacturer's instructions. Butter a soufflé dish that is 14 cm (5½ inches) in diameter and 9 cm (3½ inches) high and line the base with a circle of greaseproof paper.

2 Make the pudding base. Spoon the syrup, sugar and marmalade into the dish. Cut the bananas in half lengthways, then cut each piece in half again crossways. Toss in the lemon juice and arrange the pieces, cut side down, in the dish.

3 Make the gingerbread. Put the butter, sugar, syrup and marmalade in a saucepan and heat gently until melted. Beat the eggs and milk together in a small bowl and combine the flour, bicarbonate and ginger in another small bowl.

4 Take the pan off the heat and gradually mix in the egg and milk mixture, then the flour mixture until smooth. Pour over the bananas in the dish. Cover the top loosely with foil. Lower the dish into the slow cooker pot (see page 13). Pour boiling water into the gap between the dish and the pot so that it comes halfway up the sides of the dish, cover and cook on high for 4–5 hours or until the top springs back when pressed with a fingertip.

5 Lift out of the slow cooker, remove the foil, loosen the sides of the pudding then cover with a plate and invert on to the plate. Shake smartly to release, carefully remove the dish and peel away the lining paper. Serve with custard or vanilla ice cream

gingerbread

Poached orchard
fruits with star anise

This light fresh blend of just-cooked fruits is also delicious served chilled for breakfast, topped with spoonfuls of yogurt.

Serves 6

Preparation time: 20 minutes
Cooking time: 2½–3 hours
Cooking temperature: high
Slow cooker size: standard round or oval

100 g (3½ oz) caster sugar
300 ml (½ pint) water
3 star anise
grated rind and juice of 1 lemon
300 ml (½ pint) cranberry and raspberry juice
3 pears
2 dessert apples
400 g (13 oz) red plums
Greek yogurt drizzled with honey, to serve

1 Preheat the slow cooker if necessary – see manufacturer's instructions. Put the sugar, measured water, star anise and lemon rind and juice into a saucepan. Heat gently until the sugar has dissolved, then boil for 1 minute. Add the cranberry and raspberry fruit juice and reheat.

2 Quarter, core and peel the pears and apples and cut each apple piece in half again. Halve and stone the plums. Put the fruit in the slow cooker pot and pour over the hot syrup. Cover and cook on high for 2½–3 hours or until the fruits are tender.

3 Serve warm or cold with spoonfuls of Greek yogurt drizzled with honey.

Tip
• **Warn your diners not to eat the star anise.**

Coconut and lime rice pudding

This new twist on an old favourite is made with reduced-fat coconut milk, sugar and lime rind. Serve topped with mango slices and scoops of crème fraîche.

Serves 4

Preparation time: 15 minutes
Cooking time: 7–8 hours
Cooking temperature: low
Slow cooker size: standard round or oval

400 ml (14 fl oz) can reduced-fat coconut milk
450 ml (¾ pint) full-fat milk
15 g (½ oz) butter
75 g (3 oz) pudding rice
50 g (2 oz) caster sugar
grated rind of 2 limes

To serve

1 mango, stoned, peeled and diced
juice of 1 lime
crème fraîche

1 Preheat the slow cooker if necessary – see manufacturer's instructions. Pour the coconut milk and full-fat milk into a saucepan and bring just to the boil.

2 Butter the inside of the slow cooker pot and add the rice, sugar and lime rind. Pour the hot milk over the rice and stir to mix. Cover and cook on low for 7–8 hours, stirring once or twice if possible, until the rice is soft and has absorbed most of the milk.

3 Toss the mango pieces in lime juice. Spoon the pudding into bowls and serve topped with crème fraîche and mango.

Tips

- **This version of rice pudding is more like one cooked on the hob, so it is perfect for people who like rice pudding but who hate the skin.**

- **For a change, flavour the pudding with 3 tablespoons of set honey, a little grated nutmeg and 900 ml (1½ pints) full-fat milk instead of the mixture of coconut and dairy milk, sugar and lime.**

Poached apricots

Although adding pepper to a dessert may sound a little strange, it adds a hot spiciness that complements the dryness of the sherry. Any leftover apricots can be puréed and swirled through Greek yogurt for a tasty breakfast.

Serves 4

Preparation time: 5 minutes
Cooking time: 3–4 hours
Cooking temperature: low
Slow cooker size: standard round or oval

300 g (10 oz) ready-to-eat dried apricots
150 ml (¼ pint) dry sherry (such as Tio Pepe)
150 ml (¼ pint) cold water
50 g (2 oz) caster sugar
½ teaspoon black peppercorns, roughly crushed
crème fraîche or vanilla ice cream, to serve

1 Preheat the slow cooker if necessary – see manufacturer's instructions. Put the apricots, sherry and measured water into the slow cooker pot. Sprinkle over the sugar and peppercorns. Cover and cook on low for 3–4 hours or until the apricots are plump and piping hot.

2 Spoon the apricots into glass tumblers and serve hot with spoonfuls of crème fraîche or vanilla ice cream.

Tip
- **You can cook fresh apricots with the same flavourings. Use 500 g (1 lb) fruit and leave whole, or halve and remove the stones if preferred. Cook for 2 hours.**

with cracked pepper

Mini coffee sponge

puddings with coffee liqueur

Serves 4

Preparation time: 30 minutes
Cooking time: 2–2½ hours
Cooking temperature: high
Slow cooker size: standard oval

100 g (3½ oz) butter, plus extra for greasing
50 g (2 oz) pecan nuts
2 teaspoons instant coffee
3 teaspoons boiling water
100 g (3½ oz) soft light muscovado sugar
2 eggs, beaten
125 g (4 oz) self-raising flour
40 g (1½ oz) dark chocolate

To serve

4 tablespoons double cream
4 tablespoons coffee cream liqueur

1 Preheat the slow cooker if necessary – see manufacturer's instructions. Lightly butter 4 metal moulds, each with a capacity of 200 ml (7 fl oz), and line the bases with circles of greaseproof paper. Arrange 3 pecan nuts in the base of each mould, then break the remaining nuts into pieces with your fingertips. Put the coffee in a cup and stir in the measured boiling water until dissolved.

2 Put the butter and sugar in a bowl and cream them together with a wooden spoon until light and fluffy. Gradually mix in alternate spoonfuls of beaten egg and flour until both have been added.

3 Stir in the broken nuts and the dissolved coffee, then spoon half the mixture into the buttered moulds. Cut the chocolate into 4 pieces and press a piece into each mould. Cover with the remaining coffee mixture and smooth the tops.

4 Cover each pudding with a piece of buttered foil and transfer the puddings to the slow cooker. Pour boiling water into the pot so that it comes halfway up the sides of the moulds, cover and cook on high for 2–2½ hours or until the tops spring back when pressed with a fingertip.

5 Turn out the puddings into shallow bowls, remove the lining paper and spoon the cream and liqueur around the bases.

Tip
- **For a double chocolate pudding, replace 1 tablespoon flour with 1 tablespoon cocoa powder and omit the dissolved coffee.**

Hot toddies

Hot Mexican coffee

A mix of cocoa, coffee and rum is spiked with a red chilli. Serve as it is or topped with a spoonful of lightly whipped cream and a dusting of cocoa or grated chocolate.

Serves 4

Preparation time: 10 minutes
Cooking time: 3–4 hours
Cooking temperature: low
Slow cooker size: standard round or oval

50 g (2 oz) cocoa powder
4 teaspoons instant coffee
1 litre (1¾ pints) boiling water
150 ml (¼ pint) dark rum
100 g (3½ oz) caster sugar
½ teaspoon ground cinnamon
1 large dried or fresh red chilli, halved

To decorate

150 ml (¼) pint double cream
2 tablespoons grated dark chocolate,
4 small dried chillies (optional)

1 Preheat the slow cooker if necessary – see manufacturer's instructions. Put the cocoa and instant coffee in a bowl and mix to a smooth paste with a little of the boiling water.

2 Pour the cocoa paste into the slow cooker pot, add the remaining boiling water, the rum, sugar, cinnamon and red chilli and mix together.

3 Cover and cook the toddy on low for 3–4 hours until piping hot or until required. Stir well, then ladle it into heatproof glasses. Whip the cream until it is just beginning to hold its shape and spoon a little into each glass. Decorate each drink with a little grated chocolate and a dried chilli, if using.

Tip
• **Use level teaspoons of coffee or the flavour will be too overpowering.**

Honeyed cider
and spiced apple

Put this on to cook while you find your boots and coats, then lower the temperature just as you go out for a weekend walk. It's a welcome treat to come back to and a change from the heavier, red-wine based versions.

Serves 6

Preparation time: 10 minutes
Cooking time: 4–5 hours
Cooking temperature: high and low
Slow cooker size: standard round or oval

2 dessert apples
12 cloves
2 cinnamon sticks
75 g (3 oz) set honey
1 litre (1¾ pints) vintage dry cider

1 Preheat the slow cooker if necessary – see manufacturer's instructions. Core each apple and cut it into thick slices. Press the cloves into 12 apple slices and put them in the slow cooker pot.

2 Break the cinnamon sticks in half and add them to the apples with the honey and cider.

3 Cover and cook on high for 1 hour, then reduce the temperature to low for 3–4 hours or until piping hot. You can cook this toddy for longer if liked. Stir well and ladle into heatproof glasses to serve.

Tip

• **If you have some calvados (apple brandy), you might like to add a little to the toddy just before serving.**

Hot citrus burst

Serves 6

Preparation time: 10 minutes
Cooking time: 4–5 hours
Cooking temperature: high and low
Slow cooker size: standard round or oval

8 cardamom pods
rind of 1 lemon and juice of 3 lemons
rind of 1 orange and juice of 3 oranges
125 g (4 oz) set honey
100 g (3½ oz) caster sugar
750 ml (1¼ pints) cold water
150 ml (¼ pint) whisky

1 Preheat the slow cooker if necessary – see manufacturer's instructions. Crush the cardamom pods using a pestle and mortar or with the end of a rolling pin and put the pods and seeds into the slow cooker pot.

2 Add the fruit rinds and juice, honey, sugar, water and whisky. Cover and cook on high for 1 hour, then reduce the temperature to low for 3–4 hours, until piping hot, or longer if liked. Stir well and ladle into small, heatproof glasses.

Apricot and brandy ratafia

Serves 6

Preparation time: 15 minutes
Cooking time: 3–4 hours
Cooking temperature: low
Slow cooker size: standard round or oval

1 teaspoon sunflower oil
40 g (1½ oz) flaked almonds
100 g (3½ oz) ready-to-eat dried apricots
1 litre (1¾ pints) white grape juice
150 ml (¼ pint) brandy
75 g (3 oz) caster sugar

1 Preheat the slow cooker if necessary – see manufacturer's instructions. Heat the oil in a frying pan, add the almonds and cook, stirring, until golden all over.

2 Add the almonds and apricots to the slow cooker and pour in the grape juice and brandy. Add the sugar, cover and cook on low for 3–4 hours until piping hot or until required. Stir well and ladle into heatproof glasses to serve.

Hot Jamaican punch

Serves 6

Preparation time: 10 minutes
Cooking time: 3–4 hours
Cooking temperature: high and low
Slow cooker size: standard round or oval

juice of 3 limes
300 ml (½ pint) dark rum
300 ml (½ pint) ginger wine
600 ml (1 pint) cold water
75 g (3 oz) caster sugar

To decorate

1 lime, thinly sliced
2 slices of pineapple, cored but skin left on and cut
   into pieces

1 Preheat the slow cooker if necessary – see manufacturer's instructions. Strain the lime juice into the slow cooker pot and discard the pips. Add the rum, ginger wine, water and sugar, cover and cook on high for 1 hour.

2 Reduce the heat to low and cook for 2–3 hours until the punch is piping hot or until you are ready to serve. Stir well, then ladle into heatproof glasses and add a slice of lime and 2 pieces of pineapple to each glass.

Grossmutter's punch

Serves 8

Preparation time: 5 minutes
Cooking time: 3–4 hours
Cooking temperature: high and low
Slow cooker size: standard round or oval

750 ml (1¼ pints) red wine (75 cl bottle)
600 ml (1 pint) cold water
150 ml (¼ pint) dark rum
1 'breakfast tea' teabag
125 g (4 oz) caster sugar
6 cinnamon sticks, to serve

1 Preheat the slow cooker if necessary – see manufacturer's instructions. Pour the wine, measured water and rum into the slow cooker pot. Add the teabag and sugar, cover and cook on high for 1 hour.

2 Stir the punch and remove the teabag. Reduce the heat to low and cook for 2–3 hours until it is piping hot or until required.

3 Stir just before serving, ladle the punch into heatproof glasses and serve with a cinnamon stick stirrer.

Index

Acknowledgements

The author and publisher would like to thank Morphy Richards for loaning a range of different sized slow cookers for the testing and photography of this book. For further information, visit the Morphy Richards website on www.morphyrichards.co.uk or write to Morphy Richards, Talbot Road, Mexborough, South Yorkshire, S64 8AJ. They would also like to thank Prima for supplying a range of slow cookers for photography. For further information, write to Nu-World UK Ltd, Prima, 15 (2D) Springfield Commercial Centre, Bagley Lane, Pudsey, LS28 5LY.

Executive Editor: Sarah Ford
Editor: Charlotte Wilson
Executive Art Editor: Karen Sawyer
Designer: Miranda Harvey
Photographer: Stephen Conroy
Home Economist: Sara Lewis
Props Stylist: Rachel Jukes
Senior Production Controller: Manjit Sihra

Special photography:
© Octopus Publishing Group Limited/Stephen Conroy